LIFESTYLE
WORSHIP

LIFESTYLE WORSHIP

ORLANDO FIGUEIREDO

authorHOUSE®

AuthorHouse™ UK Ltd.
1663 Liberty Drive
Bloomington, IN 47403 USA
www.authorhouse.co.uk
Phone: 0800.197.4150

Published by AuthorHouse   06/16/2014

ISBN: 978-1-4969-8384-8 (sc)
ISBN: 978-1-4969-8385-5 (e)

Library of Congress Control Number: 2014910827

CONTENTS

LIFESTYLE WORSHIP INTRODUCTION

This study guide addresses the question: "What is a lifestyle of worship and how do I become a worshipper?" The Father seeks those who will worship Him in Spirit and Truth, what does this mean? What defines a worshipper? Is it my church attendance on Sunday or the songs that I sing? Is church the only place where I am to worship God?

The cry of Gods heart today is for intimacy with His children; worship is the doorway to a life of intimacy with God. King David discovered this key very early in his life and it served him well. He was a worshipper first and foremost in his life, being King over God's people came in second. He had a very deep and profound love for his God, it was out of this love that he worshipped and served God as a King over God's people. He became a King not because of any leadership abilities he may have possessed, but because he had a right heart before God whom he loved.

The attitude of the heart is what will open doors and not who we are or what abilities we may possess. King David ticked all the boxes, his life revolved around worshipping God and expressing his love for Him continually, regardless of the opinion of man. This ultimately saw him usher in a new era of worship in Israel when he set up his own tabernacle, and introduced a worship based on love not ceremony. The spirit of the tabernacle of David lives on today in the hearts of every believer who loves God, and who is not ashamed to express that love and become the expression of God's love to this world.

We are a Royal Priesthood before God; we are Priests under a New Covenant called to minister before the Throne of Grace as we lift up our praises to our God and King. This is the call on the life of every child of God today, to stand daily in His presence and worship the Lord who has given us eternal life. We not only have redemption through Christ and hence a place in heaven, but we have received a ministry as well; to minister to the heart of the Father. How we fulfil this ministry is the subject of this book.

You will learn that praise has a variety of expressions and we will look at six of these expressions of praise. We will also look at thanksgiving which forms a very important part of our lives and should not be over looked. I personally have seen my life transformed as I have embraced these principles and applied them to my life on a daily basis, allowing the Holy Spirit to flow His life through me continually as I now abide in His presence and love. It is my hope that everyone reading this book would also see their lives transformed to the glory of God.

All scriptures and word studies used in this study guide are from the New American Standard Bible and the New American Standard Exhaustive Concordance.

We are instructed by the Scriptures to meditate on the Word of God rather than simply study the Word of God, Ps1. The reason for this is to allow God to reveal the meaning of His Word rather than me trying to reason out its meaning, using my limited knowledge and wisdom. I would encourage you to meditate on the scriptures presented, opening your heart to the leading of the Holy Spirit to enlighten you with His meaning of the scriptures relative to your life. All of God's scriptures revolve around life not knowledge for the sake of acquiring knowledge, for only then will lives be transformed by the power of the Holy Spirit.

This study guide has been written in a workbook format, for use by both individuals and study groups, having space for the recording of personal insights and answers. Our primary teacher is the Holy Spirit who enlightens our hearts and minds with His truth about life and our walk with God. You are encouraged therefore, to seek His wisdom and truth for your life while reading this study guide. The goal of this book is to have an encounter with God and not to merely acquire more knowledge. Pray, seek, meditate, open your heart and God will fill it with His good pleasure.

CHAPTER ONE

Intimacy – The Desire of God's Heart

"And after He had removed him, He raised up David to be their king, concerning whom He also testified and said, 'I HAVE FOUND DAVID the son of Jesse, A MAN AFTER MY HEART, who will do all My will.' Acts 13:22

Intimacy – the Desire of God's Heart

In 'Lifestyle Worship' we will examine the life of a worshipper, and the call and desire of God's heart towards His people whom He has redeemed and called by His name. Worship is something many misunderstand; believing it is something we do in church on Sunday and hence has become the definition of worship for many. Nothing could be further from the truth since worship is not something I do, but something I become, I become a worshipper, and my entire life becomes an expression of my love and adoration by the power of the Holy Spirit flowing through me.

Worship is not something I do, it's something I become.
I become a Worshipper
Principle: The heart of the Father cries out for intimacy with His children.

God is seeking a very specific type of worship, one based on intimacy with Him. He does not seek ceremonial type worship; which takes one through the motions of worship but which releases no life in the believer. Worship based on intimacy with God will release the love, power and anointing of God in one's life. As we enter into the presence of God so we are touched and transformed by His presence, as we come face to face with our redeemer and lover of our soul, and we see God for who He is.

To be intimate with God is to know God and be one with God. Jesus has set us free from the power of sin, which has separated man from God since the fall of Adam and Eve in the Garden of Eden. We have been redeemed and reunited with the Father, as He has adopted us as sons and given us His Holy Spirit, by whom we now cry 'Abba! Father' (Rom 8:15). God has once again breathed His life (character, nature, strength, wisdom and provision), into man so that we now live by the Spirit walking with God in communion with Him as one. Rightly did the Apostle Paul say " I have been crucified with Christ; and it is no longer I who live, but Christ lives in me; and the life which I now live in the flesh I live by faith in the Son of God, who loved me and gave Himself up for me." Galatians 2:20.

What this means for every Christian is God is not so far away as to leave us on our own, no, God is one with us and in us, and we may now abide in His very presence continually, experiencing God in our lives as we live with open hearts towards Him. He is not a million miles away in heaven somewhere, but He has chosen to dwell with man by His Spirit so we may experience His life flow within us on a daily basis.

John 17:11 NASB

> "And I am no more in the world; and yet they themselves are in the world, and I come to Thee. Holy Father, keep them in Thy name, the name which Thou hast given Me, that they may be one, even as We are.

Intimate worship = The expression of my heart in response to the abiding presence of God in my life.

Q1. How might the presence of God touch your life each day?

_____

Ceremonial worship may be described as going through the motions to appease our conscience out of a sense of duty.

Q2. How would one become a ceremonial worshipper?

_____

Principle: Worship is not an activity; it's an expression of the heart.

John 4:20-24

> *"Our fathers worshiped in this mountain, and you people say that in Jerusalem is the place where men ought to worship." Jesus said to her, "Woman, believe Me, an hour is coming when neither in this mountain, nor in Jerusalem, shall you worship the Father." You worship that which you do not know; we worship that which we know, for salvation is from the Jews.* **"But an hour is coming, and now is, when the true worshipers shall worship the Father in spirit and truth; for such people the Father seeks to be His worshipers."** *God is spirit and those who worship Him must worship in spirit and truth.*

Time and location then do not define worship but the attitude and expression of your heart in the presence of God. God seeks those who are led by His Spirit, who will walk in revelation according to His Word and who openly express their love for Him.

What defines worship?

The attitude and expression of my heart in response to the presence of God

Worship is an attitude of the heart which a believer expresses daily in his walk with God. Worship is not restricted to a particular location or time, but may be freely entered into as one opens one's heart to our Sovereign God, to both love and be loved. God loves to hear us express our love for Him and is moved by our open heart towards Him as we express our love for Him.

Key to worship is an open heart before God
An open heart can be defined by: our heart attitude.

HEART ATTITUDE + EXPRESSION OF THE HEART = THE PRESENCE OF GOD

Q3. What heart attitude might you have each day towards God?

_____

Q4. God loves to hear us express our heart to Him.

How might you express your heart each day?

___

The Heart Expressed in Worship

Principle: A Worshipper expresses the heart of the Father

Acts 13:22

> *"And after He had removed him, He raised up David to be their king, concerning whom He also testified and said, 'I HAVE FOUND DAVID the son of Jesse, A MAN AFTER MY HEART, who will do all My will.'*

King David was a man who honoured God in everything he did, who chose to live and do things God's way. He was a man who had the utmost trust in his God and who never trusted in his own strength but relied totally on God for guidance, deliverance, protection and provision. He was a man who honoured God and was not afraid to openly express his love for God and to seek His presence.

In contrast King Saul had been a self-willed individual, who did not hesitate in taking matters into his own hand and was disobedient to Gods commands. He never expressed any love for God as did King David, instead he became a self-serving King; a characteristic which cost him his throne. (1Sam 13:11-14)`

God seeks those who will seek His presence and become one with Him, being transformed into His glorious image; that our lives may become the expression and manifestation of God through our lives, as the Spirit flows from within us to accomplish all that is on the Father's heart.

Q5. Read 1Chron 16:7 – 36

Make a list of King David's heart attitudes and expressions of worship towards God.

___

Definition of a Worshipper

King David was a worshipper; one who knew God, whose heart was open and submitted to God to do all His will, and one who was not ashamed to openly express his love for God. A worshipper is one who will honour God with his life in all he does and all he is, while expressing his love unashamedly. He will give God the place of receiving the highest honour in his life by submitting his all to God as his sovereign Lord. A worshipper is one who continually experiences and walks in the presence of God and knows Him as Father and is unashamed in expressing his love for the Father.

Intimacy in Worship

Principle: Worship is the sharing of love together

John 5:19-20

> *Jesus therefore answered and was saying to them, "Truly, truly, I say to you, the Son can do nothing of Himself, unless it is something He sees the Father doing; for whatever the Father does, these things the Son also does in like manner." For the Father loves the Son, and shows Him all things that He Himself is doing; and greater works than these will He show Him, that you may marvel.*

God longs to reveal His heart to each one of His children. Worship is what will touch and open up the heart of the Father to each one of us.

Worship is the key to a life of intimacy with God as our Father

A worshipper is one who loves God, lives in the presence of God and walks in all that God reveals to him. Worship becomes an experience of great intimacy with God as we open our hearts to God, and He responds by opening His heart towards us. It is as we share love together that He fills us with His love, joy, peace, patience, kindness, goodness, faithfulness, gentleness and self-control (Gal 5:22-23).

I am transformed into the Image of Christ as He reveals Himself to me.
I open my heart by acknowledging and loving God and He responds by opening His heart and revealing himself to me.

Psa 46:10 NASB

> *"Cease striving and know that I am God; I will be exalted among the nations, I will be exalted in the earth."*

Some versions of the Bible have: "Be still and know that I am God".

Heb 12:2 NASB

> *fixing our eyes on Jesus, the author and perfecter of faith, who for the joy set before Him endured the cross, despising the shame, and has sat down at the right hand of the throne of God.*

In this verse we can see how we are meant to live our lives; with our eyes firmly fixed on Jesus. This speaks not of our natural eyes, but the eyes of our hearts, our spiritual eyes, for we are now to live our lives by continually presenting to God all of our faculties for God to flow through by His Spirit, that we might walk as one through all of life.

Q6. How may I open my heart to the Father?

Q7. What might God reveal to you as you worship Him?

_____

Q8. What might you say to God as you open your heart towards Him?

_____

Based on these three scriptures God is looking for those:

a. Who have a heart after God to do all His will.
b. Who will worship Him in Spirit and truth; living Spirit led lives according to the revelation we have in Christ.
c. Who will become one with the Father; living out of His presence and sharing love with Him.

Summary

1. Worship is not something I do, it is something I become; I become a worshipper living my life with a continual open heart towards God.
   My life becomes an expression of my love and trust in God as I honour and respect Him above all others, and in all things in my life.
2. Worship is defined by the attitude and expression of my heart in the presence of God.
3. Worship will release the flow of the Holy Spirit in my life, transforming me into the image of God.

Expressions of Worship

Definition of 'Worship' according to the Collins dictionary:

• To show profound religious devotion to; adore or venerate (a deity).
• To have intense love and admiration for.

Definition of 'Venerate' and 'Veneration' according to the Collins dictionary:

• To hold (someone) in deep respect.
• A feeling or expression of awe or reverence.

Worship then is the heart attitude of submission to and honouring God as our Father and expressing our intense love and profound respect we have for the Lord our God. It is an attitude which must in essence be expressed through our lives each and every day. Worship in its fullness will never be experienced until it is expressed through out lives.

How I choose to express this attitude can have many and varied forms since worship as we have seen is not confined to either time or location. My life then becomes a platform for expressing my worship of God and which according to John 4:23 is also Spirit led. I become a worshipper as my life becomes an expression of my heart attitude towards God, and as I chose to continually live a Christ-conscious life, living my life out of the presence of God.

Worship may be expressed in many different forms. The remainder of this module will look at these different forms of expression as we find them in the scriptures. The two principle forms we will examine are; thanksgiving and praise. Each of these will introduce you to a great variety of forms of expressions of worship; your love and adoration of God in your life.

The object of thanksgiving and praise is not only to be an expression of the attitude of your heart, but also to take you into and keep you in the abiding presence of God.

Personal Testimony

When I first came to know Christ I lived a life full of joy in the knowledge that I was saved, it was a time in my life of great rejoicing. There was nothing I would not do for Jesus; I would witness with a passion, I would attend every meeting that was going as I was hungry for more of His word in my life. As I grew in the Word so too I began to climb the leadership ladder, until I became an Elder and then the Assistant Pastor in our church, being responsible for; outreach, ushering, leading a home-cell group and preaching in our church. I was very much service orientated, serving God with all of my heart. The cry of my heart had been "Lord, use me!" This the Lord certainly did over a period of ten years from the time I was born again until I left my country of birth, Zimbabwe, to live in Australia.

For many Christians, my life would probably exemplify the life many may aspire to live. I had lived my life to serve and please God, but I had not yet learnt to live my life to love Him. This was to be the second stage of my life in Christ; learning to love Him.

So the next stage of my walk with Jesus was taken up with learning what it means to be a worshipper, and returning to my first love, something I had forgotten in my quest for service. I learnt that we are engaged to Christ and will one day be married to Him in the 'Marriage Feast of the Lamb.' So we are engaged to Christ and are living in a time of romance or courtship. It's a time of getting to know one another, a time to fall in love and share love with each other. It's a time of intimacy. Jesus made this very clear when He spoke to Martha in Luke 10:38-42

> *"Now as they were travelling along, He entered a certain village; and a woman named Martha welcomed Him into her home. And she had a sister called Mary, who moreover was listening to the Lord's word, seated at His feet. But Martha was distracted with all her preparations; and she came up to Him, and said, "Lord, do You not care that my sister has left me to do all the serving alone? Then tell her to help me." But the Lord answered and said to her, "Martha, Martha, you are worried and bothered about so many things; but only a few things are necessary, really only one, for Mary has chosen the good part, which shall not be taken away from her."*

Martha was motivated by a list of things to do, Mary was motivated by the person she spent time with; Jesus. Mary sat at Jesus' feet, looking into His eyes, seeing His love and feeling His love. She opened her heart to Jesus and took the time to find out what was on Jesus' heart and her life was enriched. Mary took the time to find out who the real Jesus was, to see and feel His heart. This would have touched Mary's mind, will and emotions in a way no list of rules, commands, or list of things to do could ever have touched her. Jesus went on to say that there is really only one thing that is necessary for us; to live our lives in His presence and out of His presence.

We live our lives with Jesus, not for Jesus.

If I live my life for Jesus it's me in action, I am a Martha

If I live my life with Jesus its Jesus in action, I am a Mary.

It's not what you do with your life, but who you spend it with!

You choose! Either rush around doing things for Jesus, or spend time with Jesus and do things with Jesus.

Worship will open the door to living with Jesus and doing things with Jesus. This is the heart of the Gospel of Jesus Christ, we are called not just be believe and receive salvation, but to know God and become as one and live as one with God, just as Jesus was one with the Father (John 17: 3 & 11).

Jesus did nothing out of His own initiative, except what He saw the Father doing! He was as one with the Father, and the Holy Spirit flowed through His life revealing the Father to the world. This is what the Father desires and longs for, to walk with His children in this life, communing and sharing love together as one. Worship is the door which opens my heart to allow God to flow through my life as one by His Spirit.

The two crucial elements the Lord added to my life was;

    a.   Learning to love Him as a worshipper.
    b.   Learning how to hear His voice and live out of His voice.

Learning to become a worshipper has transformed my life, I have returned to my first love. I now experience His love and peace every day and I walk with an anointing I had never experienced before. I have come to know my God so much more intimately now and see Him as the lover of my soul, walking daily with me through life, flowing His love, strength and wisdom by His Spirit so that we are one in all things, at all times.

Recap – What Principles have we learnt in this lesson?

    1. The heart of the Father cries out for intimacy with His children.
    2. Worship is not an activity; it's an expression of the heart.
    3. Worship is the sharing of love together.
    4. A Worshipper expresses the heart of the Father.

CHAPTER TWO

Thanksgiving in Old Testament Times

I will give thanks to Thee, O LORD, among the peoples; And I will sing praises to Thee among the nations. Ps 105:1

Life can be very complex or it can be very simple, the choice lies with me. I can make it complex as I focus my eyes on the world around me and all the issues of life, or I can choose to fix my eyes on Jesus; the author and finisher of my faith and hence my life, and look at life from God's perspective. Life can be fun, exciting, invigorating, challenging and creative, or it can be boring, frustrating, lacking direction and leaving me with a sense of hopelessness. The choice is mine.

The same can be said about my Christian walk with the Lord. I can choose to develop my love walk, or I can stagnate and never reach my full potential. Every investor knows that unless he is prepared to invest in something he will never be able to reap any financial rewards.

For the Christian this investment is worship. I must be prepared to invest heavily in worship, for only then can I expect to reap the reward of an intimate relationship with God, which will give me an abundant life. For me to be able to enjoy an intimate relationship with my heavenly Father, I must invest my time and energy to have fellowship with the Father, the Son and the Holy Spirit. Worship becomes the conduit for fellowship. Investment is generally a long term process. An investor does not invest today and tomorrow cash in his investment, and expect a big return. No he leaves his investment and does not touch it for a period of time. Worship is the same; we do not worship one day and not the next. Worship is ongoing and never ending, it becomes a part of me, who I am, and the very fabric of my life is worship.

In this lesson we begin to take a look at some of the elements that make up worship, which will become a permanent part of my life and which makes up my investment.

The Abundant Life

John 10:10

> "The thief comes only to steal, and kill, and destroy; I came that they might have life, and might have it abundantly.

The Father has invested what was most precious to Him; His Son, Jesus. The Father paid a very high price for our souls. We have been redeemed by the precious blood of the lamb. This high price should not be taken lightly, nor should the willingness of Jesus to be the ultimate sacrifice for you and me. He paid a high price so that you and I may today enjoy God's abundant life. Our abundant life has come with a very high price tag; do you really appreciate what God has done for you?

Soon after I was born again the Lord showed me, one day while in my bath, an image of what he had done for me in my life. As I pulled the bath plug and the dirty water began to disappear down the plug hole, the Lord likened this to what He had done for me on the cross. All my filth and dirt in the form of sin had been removed and washed away, never to be seen again. I was now clean and pure in the sight of God, just as the bath water had washed and cleansed me. I gained a fresh perspective and appreciation for my salvation. I saw in a moment what Jesus had done for me and I was grateful for it. Today I enjoy His abundant life because of what He did for me; never will I ever be the same again.

How can I ever repay Jesus what He did for me?

This is a question each one of us must ask ourselves.

There can be only one response for one who has experienced salvation; to give thanks. The giving of thanks is taught in both the new and old testaments as something which should be a part of our everyday lives. The giving of thanks for our salvation and the abundant life we now have is the most fundamental response, yet it is of great importance for us to understand its place in our worship experience.

Giving Thanks in Old Testament Times

The giving of thanks meant more than just saying 'Thank you.' It was not only an expression of gratitude, but a declaration and testimony of what had been done for all to hear. One would draw attention to the other person and make known what they had done for him; they would 'Tell of His name.' Today this is known as witnessing, or being a witness for Christ, We tell others of the great things God has done for us through salvation, and how great He is.

1. Giving Thanks was a time of Proclamation and Declaration.

We proclaim and declare the great name of our King and Saviour, Jesus Christ, and we proclaim the things He has done in our lives. God touches the lives of His people in so many different ways; to some He may bring physical or emotional healing, He may give us peace even when we may be facing difficult times, He gives wise counsel to those who seek it, showing them how to live a Godly life in an ungodly world. He restores His provision and blessings and gives us rest. He opens doors which no man can open and gives us favour with man. He gives us dreams and visions, inspiring us to be leaders among the nations.

The list of what God has done and will do for us is endless, and must be proclaimed that He may be honoured among His people and the nations of the world. There will always be something we can declare of our God in giving thanks to Him. The following scriptures help to illustrate this.

Psa 26:6-7 NASB

> *I shall wash my hands in innocence, And I will go about Thine altar, O LORD, That I may proclaim with the voice of thanksgiving, And declare all Thy wonders.*

Q1. What wonders might David the Psalmist be thinking of?

- Consider his persecution by King Saul and how God delivered David? (Kings 1&2)
- Israel's miraculous deliverance from Egypt. (Exodus 2-15)
- God's abundant blessings on the Nation of Israel.
- God's righteous acts among Israel.

Q2. What wonders might you want to declare and proclaim in your life in thanksgiving to God?

_____

Psa 44:8 NASB

In God we have boasted all day long, And we will give thanks to Thy name forever. Selah.

Psa 79:13 NASB

So we Thy people and the sheep of Thy pasture will give thanks to Thee forever; To all generations we will tell of Thy praise.

Psa 105:1 NASB

Oh give thanks to the LORD, call upon His name; Make known His deeds among the peoples.

Psa 108:3 NASB

I will give thanks to Thee, O LORD, among the peoples; And I will sing praises to Thee among the nations.

Q3. How should we give thanks?

_____

We declare and boast of all God has done; His mighty miracles, His power to deliver, His majesty. We do this where ever we may be, with all peoples and especially when we come together as the church, as one body.

2. Thanks given as an offering to the Lord.

Jer 33:11 NASB

the voice of joy and the voice of gladness, the voice of the bridegroom and the voice of the bride, the voice of those who say, "Give thanks to the LORD of hosts, For the LORD is good, For His loving-kindness is everlasting"; and of those who bring a thank offering into the house of the LORD. For I will restore the fortunes of the land as they were at first,' says the LORD.

Thanksgiving is an offering to God just as the giving of our finances is an offering to God. Both are important and vital in our worship experience. Our motive for the giving of our finances in our offerings should be one of giving thanks to the Lord with a heart attitude of honouring God in all things.

My thanksgiving becomes the expression of my heart, the expression of my love for my God and Father; whether it is the fruit of my lips or the giving of my finances, it is an offering to God.

Remember worship is: The attitude of the heart expressed in the presence of God.

My attitude is one of honouring God which I express by giving thanks as I stand in the presence of God.

3. Giving thanks ministered to the Lord.

1 Chr 16:4 NASB

> *And he appointed some of the Levites as ministers before the ark of the LORD*, *even to celebrate and to thank and praise the LORD God of Israel:*

These Levite priests no longer offered up animal sacrifices, instead they ministered to the Lord by celebrating His goodness with thanksgiving and praise. This was unheard of in the history of Israel. It was a new day; a new era had been ushered in.

Thanksgiving is to be considered as personal ministry unto the Lord. We are all called to be ministers and as the Kings priests; we minister directly to the heart of the Father as we stand in His presence and praise Him with a grateful heart. To think that you and I are able to minister to God; the one who is able to do all things that we can think or even imagine, the one who created the worlds and everything in it, the one who created man in His own image and likeness, and the one who has all the power, wisdom and knowledge. The one, who has need of nothing material since He created it all, is the same one who longs for intimate fellowship with us, who seeks our attention and love, who seeks to be acknowledged as our creator with a simple 'Thank you'. Yes, a simple thank you will bless the heart of the Father and open up His heart toward us.

Note how one ministers to the heart of the Father;

- Celebrating
- Thanking
- Praising

We minister by celebrating our freedom and rejoicing in it, by celebrating the Lord our God; we celebrate His goodness, His power to deliver, His presence in our lives, His holiness, His everlasting loving kindness. We celebrate '**WHO HE IS!'**

We minister by thanking God for directing our every footstep, for setting us free from sin and the bondage of sin, for protecting us, for providing for us, for our every well-being.

WE MINISTER BY <u>**SEEKING**</u> HIM DAILY!

In seeking His wisdom, His direction, His provision, His strength, His power, HIS VOICE for our lives, we celebrate the Lord our God.

Q4. Discuss the different ways you might bring a thank offering to God.

_____

4. Giving thanks was continually given in abundance.

Thanksgiving was something which was ingrained and etched into the life of King David; it became a part of the very fabric and make up of his life. In my own life, hardly an hour goes by without me giving thanks for something that is happening in my life. We must live with our God in the present and not just the future or past. He is with us continually seeking to direct our steps and bless our lives in some way.

Many times we take credit for something we have done, believing it is our own wisdom or skill in some area which has gone favourably for us, yet it is God directing your steps that He may be glorified in your life, in all that you do!

1 Chr 23:30 NASB

And they are to stand every morning to thank and to praise the LORD, and likewise at evening,

Psa 109:30 NASB

With my mouth I will give thanks abundantly to the LORD; And in the midst of many I will praise Him.

Psa 45:17 NASB

I will cause Thy name to be remembered in all generations; Therefore the peoples will give Thee thanks forever and ever.

We have been called to a life of ministering to God, and not just receiving all His blessing and promises. It is to be a **life** of ministering, not a Sunday of ministering.

Just as the Levite priests in the Old Testament ministered daily and just as David appointed them to minister before the Ark every day, so we too must stand before God every day and minister to the heart of the Father.

Have you ministered to the Father's heart today?

The Lord spoke to me one day in my prayer time and said;

"Lift up your voice and praise Me continually son, this is your call son to worship Me always."

Thanksgiving should never be far from our lips and we should seek to continually honour the Lord with it. Thanksgiving should be an overflowing gratitude towards God, expressed with the fruit of our lips. Silence cannot thank nor praise God, but it is only as we open our mouths and begin to proclaim and declare His goodness as the expression of our hearts.

Q5. Consider how you will minister to God today, tomorrow and the next?

_____

5. Giving thanks was included in prayers.

Thanksgiving should be a part of our prayer life as well, in giving thanks for what the Lord has done or is about to do. Jesus would often give thanks to His Father in His prayers. It becomes a part of our very lifestyle.

Neh 11:17 NASB

> *and Mattaniah the son of Mica, the son of Zabdi, the son of Asaph, who was the leader in beginning the thanksgiving at prayer, and Bakbukiah, the second among his brethren; and Abda the son of Shammua, the son of Galal, the son of Jeduthun.*

6. Thanksgiving is to be spontaneous

Thanksgiving began as a ceremonial act of worship in the tent of meeting as a 'Peace Offering' in the days of Moses, when one would bring his peace offering before the priest and offer it as a thank offering to the Lord.

Lev 7:13 NASB

> *'With the sacrifice of his peace offerings for thanksgiving, he shall present his offering with cakes of leavened bread.*

This ceremonial act was one not required to be presented at specific times but could be presented at any time as the giver desired in his heart. It was a spontaneous act and a picture of what was to come.

When David became King he introduced a new order of worship not seen in Israel previously; he set up a tent which became known as the 'Tabernacle of David.' The only piece of furniture to be found here was the Ark of the Covenant; indicating the presence of God.

Only once, at the initiation were burnt offerings and peace offerings brought before God, as they had been in the Tabernacle of Moses, but thereafter they brought a very different kind of offering; their offerings became songs of praise and thanksgiving. Here for the first time Israel worshipped not with the usual ceremonies, but with individual spontaneous expressions of worship in song, music and dance before the presence of the Lord.

1 Chr 16:1 NASB

And they brought in the ark of God and placed it inside the tent which David had pitched for it, and they offered burnt offerings and peace offerings before God.

1 Chr 16:5-6 NASB

Asaph the chief, and second to him Zechariah, then [a]Jeiel, Shemiramoth, Jehiel, Mattithiah, Eliab, Benaiah, Obed-edom and Jeiel, with musical instruments, harps, lyres; also Asaph played loud-sounding cymbals, 6 and Benaiah and Jahaziel the priests blew trumpets continually before the ark of the covenant of God.

1Chr 16:7 NASB

Then on that day David first assigned [a]Asaph and his [b]relatives to give thanks to the Lord.

Let us not wait for Sunday, which is recognised as the official day of worship in the church, to express your love for Jesus and offer Him thanks for being the Father's sacrificial lamb, and dying for your sins. The heart of King David was continually open to expressing his love for his God, he could think of nothing better than to spend his life praising and singing songs of praise to the lover of his soul.

Do not allow the opinions of man to hinder your ministry to the Father, but rather fix your eyes on Jesus and love the Lord with all your heart. May we all have the same heart as David had and be fearless in expressing our love for Lord.

Q6. When is it a good time to offer thanksgiving to God?

---

7. Giving thanks is a time of rejoicing.

Thanksgiving was a time of great rejoicing in the nation of Israel, and a great fan-fare was made of it.

1 Chr 16:4 NASB

And he appointed some of the Levites as ministers before the ark of the LORD, even to celebrate and to thank and praise the LORD God of Israel:

Thanksgiving is to be a time of rejoicing as we remember what great things God has done for us, our focus is on God and not on what is before us. It is a time of celebration in the presence of the Lord.

Q7. Describe how one might rejoice? Would it be a solemn occasion or an exuberant occasion, a quiet or noisy one?

---

8. Giving thanks may be offered as a sacrifice.

Psa 54:6 NASB

> *Willingly I will sacrifice to Thee; I will give thanks to Thy name, O LORD, for it is good.*

Thanksgiving does not always come easily to us, especially when we are hard pressed by situations in life which confront us. At these times it becomes a sacrifice as we choose to turn away from that which confronts us and we focus on Jesus and put our trust in Him to deliver us.

The prophet Jonah is a good example of a sacrifice of thanksgiving. He was swallowed alive by a whale as a result of his disobedience to God for not wanting to go to Nineveh and preach repentance. He had run away from the presence of the Lord. In the depths of his misery he came to his senses and repented by offering a sacrifice of thanksgiving to God for his deliverance, and making a vow to heed the command of the Lord and return to Gods holy temple. He will no longer run away from the Lord but will seek His presence. God responded by freeing him from the whale.

Jonah 2:9 NASB

> *But I will sacrifice to Thee with the voice of thanksgiving. That which I have vowed I will pay. Salvation is from the LORD." Then the LORD commanded the fish, and it vomited Jonah up onto the dry land.*

Jonah's sacrifice of thanksgiving was to praise God despite his circumstances. In the natural there was no way of escape. He knew salvation could only come from God. So he repented of his bad attitude and sought Gods presence once again by praising His name, and calling upon His name to honour God, expressing the belief that only God had the power to deliver him, and would indeed deliver him.

Jonah began to thank God for his deliverance. As he sang, his words would have stirred up faith within his heart towards God. He went from one having no hope and down cast to one having faith in His God to move mountains. The words he expressed in the sacrifice of thanksgiving produced faith in his heart for the impossible.

The following is a journal in which I asked the Lord what He had to say about Thanksgiving. A journal is my pray written down and Gods response to my prayer. I will use a number of journals throughout this study guide.

Jonah was My prophet, called to reveal My name to many. Yes his heart did fail him, he ran from My presence, but today many do the same, as I call they look only at their own abilities and shrink back from My call. This displeases Me for when I call I empower and release My gifting for the task

Many run and never see My hand upon their lives because they run away from Me. Those who run dishonour Me. Thanksgiving son is something Jonah learnt the hard way. I extended My mercy to him to save him. Thanksgiving came upon him as I revealed my hand, as I called to him in the depths of despair and he responded to me. I forgave him and this is the underlying tone of thanksgiving; I forgive and man responds to me. Jonah responded with faith in his heart, he gave Me praise in the midst of adversity and calamity. He again honoured My name. This is what set him free; he again chose to honour Me, at a time when I was his only hope. Honour son, honouring Me will always reveal My hand of mercy, love and compassion to bless My people, I must be honoured in their lives.

Q8. Identify life an occasion in your life when a sacrifice of thanksgiving might be appropriate.

A Psalm of Thanksgiving

The following psalm aptly demonstrates a heart of worship and what it means to thank and praise the Lord. It reveals the attitude of the heart of worship as one minister's to the heart of the Father. This was the worship King David introduced and which God still seeks today. It is found in 1Chronicles 16.

1Chr 16:8-15

> *Oh give thanks to the Lord, call upon His name;*
> *Make known His deeds among the peoples.*
> *Sing to Him, sing praises to Him;*
> *Speak of all His wonders.*
> *Glory in His holy name;*
> *Let the heart of those who seek the Lord be glad.*
> *Seek the Lord and His strength;*
> *Seek His face continually.*
> *Remember His wonderful deeds which He has done,*
> *His marvels and the judgments from His mouth,*
> *O seed of Israel His servant,*
> *Sons of Jacob, His chosen ones!*
> *He is the Lord our God;*
> *His judgments are in all the earth.*
> *Remember His covenant forever,*
> *The word which He commanded to a thousand generations,*

1Chr 16:23-29

> *Sing to the Lord, all the earth;*
> *Proclaim good tidings of His salvation from day to day.*
> *Tell of His glory among the nations,*
> *His wonderful deeds among all the peoples.*
> *For great is the Lord, and greatly to be praised;*

He also is to be feared above all gods.
For all the gods of the peoples are idols,
But the Lord made the heavens.
Splendor and majesty are before Him,
Strength and joy are in His place.
Ascribe to the Lord, O families of the peoples,
Ascribe to the Lord glory and strength.
Ascribe to the Lord the glory due His name;
Bring an offering, and come before Him;
Worship the Lord in holy array.

I suggest you meditate on this psalm and let God open it up to you.

Summary of Old Testament Thanksgiving

- Thanksgiving was expressed vocally and also given as a sacrificial offering to God.
- It was given in continuous abundance which ministered to the heart of God.
- It took the believer into the presence of God and produced rejoicing and celebration.
- It became a part of the believer's prayer life and lifestyle. It was to be a spontaneous response.
- It was offered out of gratitude for Gods deliverance. It was expressed to the local body of believers as well as to the unbeliever.
- Thanksgiving is a choice we make to honour God at all times for all things He has done for us. As we honour God so we are drawn into His presence and it releases the hand of God to bless us.

Q9. Describe what thanksgiving now means to you and how you might express it.

Recap: What Principles have we learnt in this lesson?

1. Giving Thanks was a time of Proclamation and Declaration.
2. Thanks were given as an offering to the Lord.
3. Giving thanks ministered to the Lord.
4. Giving thanks was continually given in abundance.
5. Giving thanks was included in prayers.
6. Thanksgiving is to be spontaneous.
7. Giving thanks is a time of rejoicing.
8. Giving thanks may be offered as a sacrifice.

Life Application

The best way to learn something new is to practice it until it becomes second nature to us. Life is to be an experience not a collection of thoughts and head knowledge. Our walk with God is no different, if He is not a part of our daily lives then all we have is a dead, boring religion. God is our creator, the one who breathed life into us, the one who died for us so He could become a part of our daily lives, walking in daily fellowship and communion with Him.

The principles you have just read must also be practiced until they become a regular part of our fellowship with God. Opening your heart up to the Lord, seeking and remaining in His presence begin with a thankful heart, one which openly rejoices in God so that our eyes may be continually fixed on Jesus, the author and perfector of our faith (Hebrew 12).

I would encourage you to include thanksgiving in your daily walk, let it become a natural part of life, so that in all things you may give thanks to the Lord.

CHAPTER THREE

Thanksgiving in New Testament Times

Through Him then, let us continually offer up a sacrifice of praise to God, that is, the fruit of lips that give thanks to His name. And do not neglect doing good and sharing; for with such sacrifices God is pleased. (Heb 13:15)

In the New Testament the concept of thanksgiving or giving thanks is much the same as in the Old Testament. The pattern of worship established by King David in his Tabernacle is the same one God seeks today in the life of every believer. The same principles still apply.

Acts 15:16 NASB

> "After these things I will return, and I will **rebuild the Tabernacle of David** which has fallen, and I will rebuild its ruins, and I will restore it, in order that the rest of mankind may seek the Lord, and all the gentiles who are called by My Name.' says the Lord, who makes these things known from of old.

One of the distinguishing characteristics of David's Tabernacle was individual worship; it demonstrated we are each called to worship the Lord as individuals. We worship corporately as a body as well as individually as we are able to come before the Lord, into His presence at any time and worship Him. Worship is no longer just a Sunday experience but an everyday experience and may be entered into at anytime and anywhere.

In the Tabernacle of David each of one of the priests was able to come before the Ark of the Covenant and freely offer his worship in the presence of the Lord. They ministered by offering thanks and praise in an atmosphere of celebration, unlike the Tabernacle of Moses which was a solemn place where animals were sacrificed, and the Ark of the Covenant accessible only once a year by the High Priest.

Principle: Worship is not just a Sunday experience but a daily experience.

Five Reasons for Thanking God

There are many reasons why we should thank God for what He is doing in our lives. The following are some of the principle reasons for offering thanksgiving today.

1. Salvation is the primary reason for giving thanks

2 Cor 4:15 NASB

> For all things are for your sakes, that the grace which is spreading to more and more people may cause the giving of thanks to abound to the glory of God.

Our salvation will always be the primary reason for the offering of thanksgiving to God. It becomes the corner stone of our worship experience. If I cannot give thanks for my salvation then what will I give thanks for?

Thanksgiving for our salvation will cause deep wells to be dug in our lives, which God will fill to overflowing with His waters of life, releasing His abundant life within us and causing many to come and seek these waters for themselves. The giving of thanks is to abound in our lives, in other words it is to be a continual and overflowing experience in our lives which must never cease. All that I say and all that I do will be the reflection of a thankful and grateful heart to God for my salvation.

Col 2:6 NASB

> *As you therefore have received Christ Jesus the Lord, so walk in Him, having been firmly rooted and now being built up in Him and established in your faith, just as you were instructed, and overflowing with gratitude.*

Q1. Does my life overflow with gratitude for my salvation?

If it does, how does it overflow?
If it doesn't how could I make it overflow?

---

2. I will tell of His name

We saw in the previous lesson the basic concept of the giving of thanks in the Old Testament. One would draw attention to the other person and make known what they had done for them; they would 'Tell of His name.' This is what evangelism is all about; 'Telling another that which Christ has done for me.'

1Pet 3:14 NASB

> *But even if you should suffer for the sake of righteousness, you are blessed. AND DO NOT FEAR THEIR INTIMIDATION, AND DO NOT BE TROUBLED, but sanctify Christ as Lord in your hearts, always being ready to make a defence to everyone who asks you to give an account for the hope that is in you, yet with gentleness and reverence;*

We must always be ready to give an account for the faith we have in Jesus Christ. Our testimony will honour Jesus and our heavenly Father, as we declare all He has done for us and how He set us free from; sin, condemnation, guilt, a poor self-image, sickness and disease etc. The list is endless of the things Christ has set us free from.

Our testimony should always be given in a spirit of gentleness and respect for the other person. Jesus came to this earth with humility not pride. I have seen too many people turned off Christianity, with whom I worked, because of the way a Christian has presented his testimony and life. Arrogance, a domineering attitude and bible bashing will quickly turn off many people. Your life must back up the words you speak. Your life is to be a demonstration of the reality of Christ in you.

Eph 4:1 NASB

> *I, therefore, the prisoner of the Lord, entreat you to walk in a manner worthy of the calling with which you have been called, with all humility and gentleness, with patience, showing forbearance to one another in love, being diligent to preserve the unity of the Spirit in the bond of peace.*

1Cor 2:4 NASB

> *And my message and my preaching were not in persuasive words of wisdom, but in demonstration of the Spirit and of power, that your faith should not rest on the wisdom of men, but on the power of God.*

This does not mean we should not be zealous in sharing our testimony, but it must be tempered with humility, gentleness and patience. We are also not to put our trust in ourselves as to what we should say, but rather in the Holy Spirit to lead us and empower us, that it may be God flowing through us in all we say and do.

Q2. Have you ever considered your testimony as being thanksgiving to God for your salvation? Take some time to write down your testimony and be prepared to share it with non-Christians.

3. We are now Priests to God.

In the Old Testament days it was the Levites who were the priests; it was they who offered up all the sacrifices to God. Today however, we are all priests before God, in fact we are Gods priests or Kingdom priests, and as such we are the ones who now offer up our sacrifices to God.

1 Pet 2:5 NASB

> *you also, as living stones, are being built up as a spiritual house for a holy priesthood, to offer up spiritual sacrifices acceptable to God through Jesus Christ.*
>
> Principle: You are now a spiritual house, a place of worship and you are the priest ministering to God.

We are now the ones responsible for making the sacrifice and offering the sacrifice as ministry to the Lord. We all have this ministry; it is not up to the Pastor, nor the worship leader in our churches to minister to God for us. We are, each one of us, responsible for this ministry, and it must be taken seriously by all.

We are being built up as a spiritual house; that is we are now vessels (2Cor 4:7) housing the glory of God, the new tabernacles of God to dwell in. We are now the ones responsible to enter into the presence of the Lord and minister to him with the sacrifice of praise and thanksgiving.

Heb 13:15 NASB

> *Through Him then, let us continually offer up a sacrifice of praise to God, that is, the fruit of lips that give thanks to His name. And do not neglect doing good and sharing; for with such sacrifices God is pleased.*

Q3. As a New Testament Priest describe your ministry.

---

4. A continual sacrifice

My worship is to be of a continual nature, abounding in quantity and quality. There is only one way for me to offer up a continual sacrifice before God; my whole way of living, my lifestyle, my life must be a sacrifice to God. God is calling me to honour Him and live a Holy life, for this I must be continually grateful.

Consider this:

- Every word I speak is to be an offering to God.
- Everything I do is to be an offering to God.
- My whole life is to be considered as ministry unto the Lord.

Psa 113:3 NASB

From the rising of the sun to its setting The name of the LORD is to be praised.

Q4. How will you offer a continual sacrifice of thanksgiving in your own life on a daily basis?

Integrating Thanksgiving into My Life

As we have seen the giving of thanks revolves around our salvation experience, hence we must give thanks daily for all God has done in saving us. We must choose to honour Him and His name every day. Keeping a good attitude or a right spirit is vital. Our correct attitude before our Father should always be one of gratitude for our salvation and for the goodness of His name.

In my life I have found it is a decision I make every morning, every day is a new day requiring a fresh sacrifice. I must first see myself as my Father sees me; without sin as I have been forgiven, without any form of condemnation as there is now no condemnation for those who are in Christ Jesus, Romans 8:1. I see myself in the image of Christ, Romans 8:29, and being one with Him and the Father, John 17:11. I see the love the Father has for me and I open my heart to Jesus, asking Him to flow through my life by His Spirit that day. I find joy begins to rise up from within me and I thank God for all He has done for me and all that He is going to do in my life.

Col 3:17

Whatever you do in word or deed, do all in the name of the Lord Jesus, giving thanks through Him to God the Father.

Two words are never far from my lips; "Thankyou Jesus" or "Thankyou Father." These two words have become a part of my daily language and dialogue with God. As I fix my eyes on Jesus I see Him in all His glory according to His Word; as one full of love, joy, peace, healing, abundant life, having all power, all knowledge, lacking nothing, creator of heaven and earth. So I begin to thank Him for revealing all this to me and I declare His goodness based on all I have seen in Him. I honour Him for all that He is.

As I see Him so I see myself, for I am now one restored to His image so I thank Him for all He has done in my life, and all He does for me each day. I thank Him and rejoice in His presence knowing that as I rejoice and thank Him so I am ministering to the heart of my Father.

As I go about my day, I keep my eyes fixed on Jesus and what I have seen and I maintain a grateful heart, living out of what I have seen. As Gods presence goes with me, people begin to sense there is something different about me, and this opens doors for me to share the good news of what Jesus has done for me, and to share how great is my God and Saviour.

The Word of God becomes very important in thanksgiving, as it is the Word which will reveal Jesus to me and who He is. As I see Him in the Word of God so I am able to offer fresh thanksgiving to him every day, based on what I have seen of Him in His word. This should become something we do regularly, as we grow in the Word so shall we grow in our thanksgiving and worship experience.

Recap: What principles have we learnt about Thanksgiving?

1. Salvation is the primary reason for giving thanks
2. Thanksgiving means "I will tell of His name."
3. We are now all Priests to God offering sacrifices.
4. We offer a continual sacrifice of thanksgiving.

Exercise

Fix your eyes on Jesus, look into His eyes and feel His love for you. Write a letter to Jesus thanking Him for your salvation. Express your feelings to Him of what salvation and freedom means for you.

Now fix your eyes on Jesus again and ask Him the following question: "Lord, what would you like to say to me about thanksgiving in my life?" Open your heart and fix your eyes on Jesus, record what He says to you.

CHAPTER FOUR

The Power of Praise

Praise the Lord!
Praise God in His sanctuary;
Praise Him in His mighty expanse;
Praise Him for His mighty deeds;
Praise Him according to His excellent greatness.
Psalm 150:1-2

We have seen that worship is an attitude of our heart and we looked at some of the characteristics of thanksgiving. In this lesson we will be looking at the expression of our hearts in praise towards God and what praise will do for us.

We have been wonderfully and fearfully created in the image of God, and our ability to express ourselves to God can be a wonderfully creative experience. There are no limits as to how I may express my feelings for my heavenly Father and Jesus my Lord and Saviour. Whilst our daily Christian walk may be one of faith, our worship experience is one of love as we share love with God. It is a love walk freely expressed through our lives and every member of our bodies. This expression of our love is made manifest through our praises; as we encounter God through His word and as we come into His presence. Praise expresses our adoration and thanksgiving.

Definition of Praise

The secular definition of praise (Collins Dictionary): The act of expressing admiration.

A biblical definition might better define praise as:

THE EXPRESSION & DECLARATION OF ALL GOD IS, ACCORDING TO THE REVELATION OF GOD IN MY HEART.

I praise Him according to the revelation I have of God in my spirit.

Praise in my life

Praise in my life has become indispensable to me; I have found it to give me strength where I had none, joy when my heart felt sorrow, a fresh outlook on life when times were tough and a blessing which money cannot buy.

The Word teaches us it is more blessed to give than it is to receive, well I can certainly vouch for this principle. As I have opened my heart to my Father and poured out my heart to Him in adoration, I have found a mighty river of life flowing back into me, a river whose depth, width and length cannot be measured, the origin of which comes from the Throne of Grace.

Praise has taught me how to express my emotions for my God, it has given me tremendous release and freedom in the spirit, and it has led me to be caught up in the spirit to see God in all His majesty and glory as I have seen Him in His word. As I learnt to express my emotions and faith to God in praise, I found things which would normally hinder my walk have dropped off my life, and left me with a whole new sense of freedom and excitement to worship the Father in spirit and truth. When we are born again by the Spirit we find great excitement in our salvation, but we have yet to learn to love the Father. Praise is a stepping stone on the journey to learning how to love God, as it develops and leads us into experiencing God in a very intimate way. I have also learnt to praise God even when I did not feel like it, since our walk is a faith walk; I have praised Him in obedience to His word which reveals Him to me by His Spirit.

A Journal on Praise

The following is a question I asked the Lord in prayer regarding praise and the answer I received.

"Lord how do you see the area of **praise** and worship being integrated into life on a daily basis?"

Praise son, which comes from your heart honours Me and releases My power and anointing to accomplish the impossible in life. Praise empowers you as it releases faith which I can move through, to move mountains. Your praise is a weapon for peace and times of war. It restores peace and releases the captive. Praise sets your heart on fire by My Spirit, it leads and empowers you for service. Praise has been under estimated by so many of My people. They do not know nor understand its power. Praise is a thing of great significance as it fixes your eyes on Me to the exclusion of all else. Enter in son and praise Me for who I am, this will reveal My image to you and you will begin to see yourself in My image. Praise sets the mind free to worship Me, to exalt My name. Praise is for a lifetime, something you do in response to what you see in Me. As My Spirit reveals My will and who I am so you shall praise Me and open your life to Me. Praise Me continually son for then your eyes shall always be fixed on Me. Rely on My Spirit to reveal truth to you, then you shall praise Me in spirit and truth. Mighty are My people as they praise Me and open their hearts in worship for then I move sovereignly among My people and set them free, empowering their lives for service. Worship has not been taught many times and is lacking in My body.

Thankyou Lord.

I can certainly testify to the power of praise in my life, as it has many times empowered me to be an overcomer in trying circumstances, it has kept my focus on Jesus allowing the anointing of the Holy Spirit to release the faith of God in my life, to walk in His strength and wisdom. It has enable me to see and experience the Lords freedom, as He revealed Himself to me as I praised Him for who He is; the Almighty El Shaddai and life giving Elohim. I have experienced what God spoke in my journal and can I can testify as did King David, "Great is the Lord, and greatly to be praised."

Twelve Reasons to Praise God

a. Praise Honours God.

> Praise son that comes from your heart **honours** Me.

To honour God is the highest call on a Christian's life. We are to love the Lord with all of our heart, soul and strength. Everything within us is to be dedicated to honouring the Lord our God. Today He is our Father and must be honoured as such. This is to be a lifestyle for us, something we do naturally every day.

Honour is very important to the Lord, He takes it very seriously. In scripture we are admonished to honour our parents, our neighbours and God. We can honour the Lord with our wealth (Prov 3:8), with our praises and with our very lives.

Deut 6:5 NASB

"And you shall love the LORD your God with all your heart and with all your soul and with all your might.

Psa 50:23 NASB

"He who offers a sacrifice of thanksgiving honours Me; And to him who orders his way aright I shall show the salvation of God."

God is pleased when we choose to honour Him despite our circumstances, when perhaps life is going against us, yet we choose to remain in faith, trusting God for victory, trusting that He is still in control and able to deliver us and thus giving thanks in all things.

b. Praise releases Gods power and anointing.

Praise son, which comes from your heart honours Me and **releases My power and anointing** to accomplish the impossible in life.

We give God the highest place in our lives when we praise Him, giving God licence to flow His life through us and manifest His presence in our lives. Praise will draw us into the conscious presence of God, where we become aware of His Majestic omnipotence in our lives and flowing through our lives. It is in the presence of God that we will find the flow of life (Jn 7:38), the flow of the Holy Spirit; His strength, His wisdom, His knowledge, His creativity, His peace which surpasses all understanding.

Psa 22:3 NASB

Yet Thou art holy, O Thou who art enthroned upon the praises of Israel.

It is as we praise God that we release His sovereignty, power and authority over our lives. God does not force His way upon us, it is only as I open my heart to Him and praise Him that God is able to flow His Spirit through my life to accomplish the impossible. We were never created to live this life on our own; we were created to share life together while being empowered by the Holy Spirit for all of life. Praise acknowledges, reinforces and releases the power of God in my life.

The apostle Paul knew this only too well, nothing could stop him from praising His God whom he loved and knew. He was a man passionate about his God and was fearless in declaring it to the world, sometimes to his detriment, yet nothing could stop him, no, not even being flogged and beaten and thrown into prison. All it did was release the power of God to act on his behalf, he offered a sacrifice of praise; He acknowledged God before man, resulting in God acknowledging Paul before man.

Acts 16:25-26 NASB

But about midnight Paul and Silas were praying and singing hymns of praise to God, and the prisoners were listening to them; and suddenly there came a great earthquake, so that the foundations of the prison house were shaken; and immediately all the doors were opened, and everyone's chains were unfastened.

Q1. Consider circumstances in life when you might need to be drawn into the conscious presence of God and experience His life flow through you.

_____

c. Praise empowers.

Praise empowers you as it releases **faith** which I can move through, to move mountains.

It takes faith to enter the presence of God, but it is also praise which releases the faith of God in your life for the supernatural. Praise will stir up the heart of the believer to faith without which it is impossible to please God (Heb 11:6). We are a supernatural people as we have the Spirit of God moving mightily within and through us.

Heb 10:22 NASB

let us draw near with a sincere heart in full assurance of faith, having our hearts sprinkled clean from an evil conscience and our bodies washed with pure water.

Praise will keep me in faith for an extended period of time, as I will see God for who He is as I praise him according to His word and name. It will keep my eyes fixed on Jesus instead of me and my abilities.

Josh 6:20 NASB

So the people shouted, and priests blew the trumpets; and it came about, when the people heard the sound of the trumpet, that the people shouted with a great shout and the wall fell down flat, so that the people went up into the city, every man straight ahead, and they took the city.

There may be times when the devil may try to stop you, it might feel like you are hitting a brick wall and are unable to make any further progress. It is at these times that you need to praise God, allowing God's faith and wisdom to arise and give birth to revelation and the authority needed to stand and see God's victory.

Q2. Discuss how you have felt after you have been praising God for a while. Should this be the norm for Christians?

_____

d. Praise is a weapon.

Your praise is a weapon for peace and times of war. It restores peace and releases the captive.

Spiritual oppression is a terrible thing and no Christian should have to endure it. During times of heaviness when we feel oppressed the best solution is to praise God. Praise will break the weapon formed against us and will set us free mentally, emotionally and physically.

2 Chr 20:21-22 NASB

> *And when he had consulted with the people, he appointed those who sang to the LORD and those who praised Him in holy attire, as they went out before the army and said, "Give thanks to the LORD, for His lovingkindness is everlasting." And when they began singing and praising, the LORD set ambushes against the sons of Ammon, Moab, and Mount Seir, who had come against Judah; so they were routed.*

Notice it was the worshippers who went out first to face the enemy, praising God as they went, the army followed behind them. As man honoured God, the Lord responded by destroying their enemy without a single sword being raised in battle.

In the natural this goes against common sense, you don't send out singers to fight an army which is armed with weapons of war. These days' singers and entertainers are only sent to the front line to entertain the troops in times of war, leaving the fighting up to the troops. I seem to remember somewhere in the bible where the Lord says 'Not by might nor by power, but by My Spirit,' says the Lord of hosts (Zech 4:6). And again the Lord says "For as the heavens are higher than the earth, So are My ways higher than your ways And My thoughts than your thoughts (Isa 55:9). It seems the Lord loves to confound the wisdom of the wise and seemingly highly intelligent people of this world, yet their ways are foolish before God. I have found my best recourse in troubling times is to simply put my trust in my God, praise him, and wait upon Him for His deliverance to be made manifest in my life. He has never failed me!!

Remember our battle is not against flesh and blood, but against principalities and rulers, against the powers, against the world forces of this darkness, against the spiritual forces of wickedness in the heavenly places (Eph 6:12).

And when you have peace and rest in your life, praise Him! For the Lord is the one who grants you peace and gives your soul rest, something which is highly sought after by those who are in the world and do not know God. Though they seek it with fine riches, they are never able to truly find it, it becomes the elusive butterfly, something they chase but are never able to capture. But God has given us peace through Christ and is therefore worthy of our everlasting praises.

e. Praise sets your heart on fire.

> Praise sets your **heart on fire** by My Spirit, it leads and empowers you for service.

Everything I do and everything I am is by the Holy Spirit who teaches me, comforts me, guides me and empowers me. As I sing with the Spirit so I shall sing forth Gods will for my life, with praise releasing Gods creative power within me to create something new. A heart set on fire by the Spirit is a heart which cannot be moved or shaken by circumstances and people. Praise will strengthen your heart enabling you to stand steadfast in your walk.

1 Cor 14:15 NASB

What is the outcome then? I shall pray with the spirit and I shall pray with the mind also; I shall sing with the spirit and I shall sing with the mind also.

Eph 5:18 NASB

And do not get drunk with wine, for that is dissipation, but be filled with the Spirit, speaking to one another in psalms and hymns and spiritual songs, singing and making melody with your heart to the Lord;

Zec 4:6 NASB

Then he answered and said to me, "This is the word of the LORD to Zerubbabel saying, 'Not by might nor by power, but by My Spirit,' says the LORD of hosts.

Q3. Read Psalm 13. Discuss how David stood steadfast in his faith?

---

f. Praise fixes your eyes on Jesus.

Praise is a thing of great significance as it **fixes your eyes on Me** to the exclusion of all else.

Whatever you fix your eyes upon is what you will become! This is no truer than with children looking to their parents as their role models. It is not uncommon to hear someone make the comment "You are just like your father/mother." Since God is our Father, if we fix our eyes on Him so shall we be in His likeness. A lifestyle of praising God will ensure we are looking in the right direction for our lives. Praise settles the soul and quiets the heart as our focus is brought back to Christ; our hope, our joy and as we begin to see Him in all His glory and power all else fades away into insignificance.

Heb 12:2 NASB

fixing our eyes on Jesus, the author and perfecter of faith, who for the joy set before Him endured the cross, despising the shame, and has sat down at the right hand of the throne of God.

As I fix my eyes on Jesus it brings me into the awareness of the presence of God in my life, something every Christian needs to practice; the presence of God. Praise is the vehicle which will take me into His presence. It is worthy to note that praise (altar of incense), was the point of entry into the presence of God in the tabernacle of the tent of meeting. Exodus 40:1-5.

Q4. As Christians we are called to abide in the presence of God on a daily basis (Jn 15:4-7). What does this tell you about praise?

---

g. Praise reveals the image of God.

> Praise Me for who I am, this **will reveal My image** to you and you will begin to see yourself in My image.

Praise leads us into the presence of God where He reveals His glory to us, and where we are transformed according to His image which we behold before us. Moses who spent much time in the presence of the Lord reflected the glory of God as his face shone with His glory, Exodus 34:29-35.

Exo 30:6 NASB

> *"And you shall put this altar in front of the veil that is near the ark of the testimony, in front of the mercy seat that is over the ark of the testimony, where I will meet with you.*

The altar of incense corresponds to our praises which we offer to God. Praise prepares the heart to receive the work of the Spirit in transforming us into the image and likeness of God. We were created in His image and we are being restored back to His image (Gen 1:26, Col 3:10).

2 Cor 3:18 NASB

> *But we all, with unveiled face beholding as in a mirror the glory of the Lord, are being transformed into the same image from glory to glory, just as from the Lord, the Spirit.*

It is as I fix my eyes on Jesus and praise Him according to His word that I will begin to see God in all His glory, and will be transformed and renewed by the power of His Spirit within me.

Q4. Discuss how praise prepares the heart to receive the work of the Spirit in transforming us into His image.

---

h. The mind is set free.

> Praise sets the **mind free** to worship Me, to exalt My name.

Life today can be very demanding both emotionally and physically of us. For many life has become a maze; complex and sometimes overwhelming as we try to juggle between family, finances and work. Peace may be elusive to some and anxiety a friend to many. However, praise is Gods key to setting us free both emotionally and physically, as it will restore peace and harmony to our lives that we may give glory to God in all things.

Phil 4:6-7 NASB

> *Be anxious for nothing, but in everything by prayer and supplication with thanksgiving let your requests be made known to God. And the peace of God, which surpasses all comprehension, shall guard your hearts and your minds in Christ Jesus.*

1 Sam 16:23 NASB

> *So it came about whenever the evil spirit from God came to Saul, David would take the harp and play it with his hand; and Saul would be refreshed and be well, and the evil spirit would depart from him.*

i. It's a lifetime ministry

Praise is to be a **lifetime** experience.

Our praises are not just for today, but it is something we will carry with us for our entire lifetime and into eternity. It is something we are to teach the next generation of Gods people that there may be no end to our praises for our God. It is our lifetime ministry to God.

Psa 78:4 NASB

> *We will not conceal them from their children, but tell to the generation to come the praises of the LORD, And His strength and His wondrous works that He has done.*

Psa 104:33 NASB

> *I will sing to the LORD as long as I live; I will sing praise to my God while I have my being.*

j. It's my response to revelation.

Praise is for a lifetime, something you do **in response to what you see in Me**.

As we spend time in the Lords presence we receive revelation of who God is; as we read His word He opens the eyes of our understanding that we might see Him in truth by His Spirit. It is by His Spirit and through His word that He makes himself known to us. It is as we open our hearts to the Spirit of God by faith, that we will see God in all His glory and splendour, and then we shall cry as do the angels:

Rev 4:8 NASB

> *And the four living creatures, each one of them having six wings, are full of eyes around and within; and day and night they do not cease to say, "HOLY, HOLY, HOLY, is THE LORD GOD, THE ALMIGHTY, WHO WAS AND WHO IS AND WHO IS TO COME."*

Our response to being in His presence and seeing Him can only be one of praise, worship and thanksgiving, enabling us to offer praises as living sacrifices. An absence of praise may indicate an absence of the awareness of the presence of God in our lives through His wonderful word and revelation. We should always respond to Gods revelations with praise.

k. Praise becomes a natural part of my life

Praise Me **continually** son for then your eyes shall always be fixed on Me.

We should seek to continually live Christ-conscious lives. Daily praise will ensure my eyes are fixed on Jesus; my hope and the one who gives me faith daily to praise Him in all things. Praise should be something we give God in abundance every day of our lives, and should never be dependent on how we feel but rather given out of obedience to His word and His revelation. Praise ensures our focus is in the right place.

When our eyes are fixed on Jesus we can better tune into the flow of the Holy Spirit within us, so we may live out of the initiative of the Father as we see and hear what the Spirit is saying. John 5:19,20,30

1 Chr 16:37 NASB

So he left Asaph and his relatives there before the ark of the covenant of the LORD, to minister before the ark continually, as every day's work required;

Psa 71:8 NAS

My mouth is filled with Thy praise, And with Thy glory all day long.

Phil 4:4 NASB

Rejoice in the Lord always; again I will say, rejoice!

1 Th 5:16-18 NAS

Rejoice always; pray without ceasing; in everything give thanks; for this is God's will for you in Christ Jesus.

Praise should be a natural part of our lives as much as breathing is a natural part of life. We were created by God with natural bodies and then filled with His life as He breathed His Spirit into man. Gen 2:7. Let us not only attend to the needs of the natural man, but also the needs of the spirit man within us.

l. Praise is a work of the Spirit.

Rely on **My Spirit** to reveal truth to you, and then you shall praise Me in **spirit and truth.**

We must rely on the Holy Spirit to guide us into all truth and lead us into worshipping the Father in spirit and truth. It is the Spirit who will reveal the heart of the Father towards us, and who will reveal the Father as He is. Praise is a work of the Spirit in our lives and should not be quenched.

2 Cor 5:7 NASB

> *for we walk by faith, not by sight—*

1 Cor 2:9-12 NASB

> *but just as it is written, "THINGS WHICH EYE HAS NOT SEEN AND EAR HAS NOT HEARD, AND which HAVE NOT ENTERED THE HEART OF MAN, ALL THAT GOD HAS PREPARED FOR THOSE WHO LOVE HIM." For to us God revealed them through the Spirit; for the Spirit searches all things, even the depths of God. For who among men knows the thoughts of a man except the spirit of the man, which is in him? Even so the thoughts of God no one knows except the Spirit of God. Now we have received, not the spirit of the world, but the Spirit who is from God, that we might know the things freely given to us by God,*

Eph 1:17-18 NASB

> *that the God of our Lord Jesus Christ, the Father of glory, may give to you a spirit of wisdom and of revelation in the knowledge of Him. I pray that the eyes of your heart may be enlightened, so that you may know what is the hope of His calling, what are the riches of the glory of His inheritance in the saints and what is the surpassing greatness of His power toward us who believe. These are in accordance with the working of the strength of His might*

Let us live with open hearts before the Lord our God, praising Him with thanksgiving that He might reveal Himself to us every day in all His glory.

Recap: What principles have we learnt about Praise?

a.   Praise Honours God.
b.   Praise releases Gods power and anointing.
c.   Praise empowers.
d.   Praise is a weapon.
e. Praise sets your heart on fire.
f. Praise fixes your eyes on Jesus.
g. Praise reveals the image of God.
h. The mind is set free.
i. It's a lifetime ministry
j. It's my response to revelation.

Exercise

1. Write your own definition of praise based on these principles and what they mean to you, asking the Holy Spirit to give you insights for your life and show you how you may integrate them into your lifestyle.

    _____

2. You may want to journal and ask the Lord; "Lord would you show me the importance of praise in my life?"

    _____

Life Application

Begin to apply your definition of praise to your life on a daily basis and be prepared to come together on Sunday for a mighty time of celebration of praise! Include thanksgiving and praise God for His various names.

CHAPTER FIVE

The Expressions of Praise

"Praise is the perfect response to all that God is within me as He reveals Himself to me."

Worship is at the very heart of the Christian faith; if God is not worshipped then what we have is a man-made religion. Faith in our hearts must be released towards God who has created us and blessed us with every good gift. Faith in our hearts links us in spirit to God who is Spirit. For us to worship God we must know Him and know who we are. We have an intimate association with God which must be expressed through our lives. Praise also may be expressed in as many different ways as the heart is able to express its self. We will now examine the different ways in which one may express one's self in worship before God, using both New and Old Testaments as our models.

Who Am I?

Have you ever wondered "Who am I? What is life all about? What is the purpose of my life?" I asked myself this question, and the answer shook me to my very core. I had been pondering the question; who is God? I knew He was the creator of heaven and earth and all things in it. I knew He loved me and died for my sins. "But who is He?" I asked myself, so I asked "Lord, who are you?" His reply was simply "I AM". In other words God was saying:

"I am the one who was and is and always will be. I am not only the creator of life, but I am life. I am everything you need for life."

2Pet 1:3 NASB

*seeing that His divine power has granted to us **everything pertaining to life and godliness**, through the true knowledge of Him who called us by His own glory and excellence.*

So my next question was "Who am I?" The response I got was:

"You are the expression of the 'I AM'".
Principle: "I am the expression of all God is!"

Please take some time to ponder on this until you get the revelation of what it means for your life! I was created to be the expression of all God is. What a phenomenal realisation. The creator of heaven and earth, the lover of my soul, wants to express all that He is through me!

Col 3:9-10 NASB

Do not lie to one another, since you laid aside the old self with its evil practices, and have put on the new self who is being renewed to a true knowledge according to the image of the One who created him

Q1. "I am the expression of all God is". Discuss what this means for your life, and how you might be the expression of God in your life?

_____

A Royal Priesthood

1 Pet 2:9 NASB

> *But you are A CHOSEN RACE, A royal PRIESTHOOD, A HOLY NATION, A PEOPLE FOR God's OWN POSSESSION, that you may* **proclaim the excellencies of Him who has called you out of darkness** *into His marvellous light;*

We have been called to be the sons of God, expressing and being the expression of all that He is; proclaiming His Excellencies. As royal priests we offer up spiritual sacrifices of praise and thanksgiving as a continual and pleasing offering to our Father, proclaiming His great and everlasting love.

> Principle: If we are to be the expression of all God is, then our praise must also express and declare all God is.

This means we must know God intimately; our ministry and our worship are borne out of intimacy with God. His Word will reveal Him to me, but I must draw near to Him in spirit. **Knowledge of the word alone will not suffice!** I must draw near and worship Him in spirit and truth.

It is only as I draw near to God that I will see Him for who He really is, then will I praise Him and my praise will express all God is! It will be a bold declaration of all He is because I have seen Him as I have drawn near to Him.

> Principle: Praise becomes the overflow of what I have seen and experienced in God and cannot be contained. My heart attitude is one of love, gratitude and awe in His presence.

Praise begins to express my heart in ministry to my Father and reveals the Father to a dying world. Do you remember the basic formula for worship?

> Worship = My heart attitude expressed in the presence of God.

The life of a worshipper must revolve around the abiding presence of God in our lives and not just the knowledge of His Word.

Since praise is such an important part of our ministry to God we must know both what praise is, and how we are to express our praise to God? We have seen what praise is; the expression and declaration of all God is. Now we will look at how we may express our hearts through praise.

Q2. What do you see in God that would make you want to proclaim His Excellency? Spend some time pondering this question and make a list.

Praise – A variety of expressions

Praise is the English word used to describe the expression of our hearts to God in worship. Unfortunately the English language does not do us any justice in describing the expression of our hearts, which can vary greatly. The Hebrew language thankfully helps us to better understand praise, showing us a variety of ways with which we can express our feelings of adoration and love for God. In this lesson we look at praise from the eyes of a Hebrew person, and what praise meant to a Hebrew.

To a Hebrew praise was a time of rejoicing and expressing himself to God by whatever means were at his disposal, this meant using his all to express his heart to God in an unashamed manner. The three principle methods of expression used were: song, music and dance. Our human bodies are instruments of praise to God. If it could have been possible to cause the stones to rise up and praise Jesus whilst on His way to Jerusalem (Lk 19:37-40), then how much more are we able to praise Him with our entire being? Salvation has given us the freedom to freely express ourselves to God, as we are now the expression of all God is!

> Principle: Praise is the perfect response to all that God is within me as He reveals Himself to me.

Praise is the expression of the intense love and adoration we have for the Lord, and which is to be expressed continually as a lifestyle and ministry. God loves to be in the midst of our praises, be the centre of our praises and feels quite at home in our praises. Indeed God is enthroned and dwells in the midst of a people of praise who will honour His name with praise.

Psa 22:3 NASB

> *Yet Thou art holy, O Thou who art enthroned upon the praises of Israel.*

We will now look at the various Hebrew words associated with praise.

HALAL – 1984b

Halal means: "to praise, celebrate, glory, sing (praise), to be boastful, to rave, to be clamorous.

> Halal expresses our love for God and who He is, and celebrates His goodness in our lives. It is the expression of love by someone who is madly in love with God and will go to extraordinary lengths to express that love.

The words 'celebrate, boastful, rave, clamour' give us an indication of the nature of this type of praise. They bring to mind the scenes one may be familiar with of supporters at a sporting event, where people are not afraid to voice their support, celebrate their victory with singing and shouting, lose their inhibitions and boast about their teams' performance. It is not a time to be timid but rather to rave boastfully and celebrate their teams' victory. It is a time when one ceases to be self-conscious of what others might think of their behaviour, they are totally consumed by the passion of expressing their delight in their team. It is a very deeply passionate time for expressing their support. The following scripture describes perfectly the nature of 'Halal' as a euphoric and exuberant experience.

Principle: In Halal praise one ceases to be self-conscious of what others might think of our behaviour, being totally consumed by the passion of expressing our love for God.

2Chr 23:12-13 NASB

When Athaliah heard the noise of the people running and praising (halal) the king, she came into the house of the LORD to the people. And she looked, and behold, the king was standing by his pillar at the entrance, and the captains and the trumpeters were beside the king. And all the people of the land rejoiced and blew trumpets, the singers with their musical instruments leading the praise (halal). Then Athaliah tore her clothes and said, "Treason! Treason!"

Q3. How were the people praising? Describe the scene as you see it.

_____

When we get the revelation of who God is, that He is the 'I AM', when we are filled with the true knowledge of who God is, and we see Him for who He is; then we will praise Him with great passion, a passion which none can quench. We too will celebrate, rave and boast on our God! We will cease to be self-conscious and become wholly Christ-conscious in our worship experience.

Q4. Would you consider it appropriate and normal for Christians today to worship in this manner?

_____

I once had a conversation with a well-known Bible teacher and conference speaker, who related his experience on one occasion whilst at a major conference. He related how during praise and worship the entire front row of pastors began to spontaneously, spin around like pirouettes, as the Spirit moved upon them. This is a typical example of a halal experience. I stated earlier that "Praise is the perfect response to all that God is within me as He reveals Himself to me." We are the expression of all that God is within us. One can no more contain the glory of God within us than one can contain an exploding bomb, something has to give, in this case it is the unashamed expression of our love for our God, and the great "I AM."

Principle: Never be ashamed of openly expressing your love for God.

There have been times when I have begun to quietly praise and worship the Lord, either on my own or in a congregation, when suddenly I see a glimpse of the Glory of God, of who He is, and I explode into a mighty roar and dance that defies all mediocrity, and I begin to unashamedly and passionateiy express that which I feel and see in my heart for my God, my Father and Saviour! This is what it means to 'Halal' the Lord; it reveals the excitement and love we have for our God.

Q4. Could you ever see yourself expressing your heart to God in this manner? Discuss what might hinder you.

Principle: The Word of God & Revelation becomes the basis of our praise.

Halal is better understood when we see it as being 'the spirit of praise' rather than the method of praise. Halal defines the 'spirit of praise.' As the spirit of truth and the spirit of revelation come upon us we will praise (halal) the Lord, with hearts filled with love for our God. Once again we can see the importance of the Word of God, as the word reveals the truth about God, and the Spirit gives us revelation of His glory. We must be a word based people, relying upon the Holy Spirit to bring revelation that we might see Him for who He is, so we may worship Him in spirit and truth.

It is only when we see God as He is that we move from a religious experience, to a life changing experience.

The following scriptures further demonstrate the 'spirit of praise' in halal praise.

2 Sam 6:12-16 NASB

> *Now it was told King David, saying, "The LORD has blessed the house of Obed-edom and all that belongs to him, on account of the ark of God." And David went and brought up the ark of God from the house of Obed-edom into the city of David* **with gladness***. And so it was, that when the bearers of the ark of the LORD had gone six paces, he sacrificed an ox and a fatling. And David was* **dancing before the LORD with all his might***, and David was wearing a linen ephod. So David and all the house of Israel were bringing up the ark of the LORD* **with shouting and the sound of the trumpet.** *Then it happened as the ark of the LORD came into the city of David that Michal the daughter of Saul looked out of the window and saw King* **David leaping and dancing before the LORD***; and she despised him in her heart.*

This scripture reveals the unashamed demonstration of King David's delight and joy in the presence of God. God is with David and his people. Both David and Israel rejoiced and celebrated the presence of God in their midst with gladness, shouting, trumpets, leaping and dancing. David did not hold anything back but publicly expressed his love and joy for the Lord.

This is the spirit of Halal praise, and one which we as Christians must embrace, just as King David freely expressed his heart so must we as we serve the King of kings and the Lord of lords, He deserves nothing less. Halal is the spirit of praise in expressing our love for God.

Halal occurs frequently in connection with public worship.

Psa 22:22 NASB

> *I will tell of Thy name to my brethren; In the midst of the assembly I will praise (halal) Thee.*

Psa 35:18 NASB

> *I will give Thee thanks in the great congregation; I will praise (halal) Thee among a mighty throng.*

Psa 107:32 NASB

> *Let them extol Him also in the congregation of the people, And praise (halal) Him at the seat of the elders.*

Psa 109:30 NASB

> *With my mouth I will give thanks abundantly to the LORD; And in the midst of many I will praise (halal) Him.*

Halal type of praise should be a natural part of our congregational worship services, as we allow the anointing of the Holy Spirit to empower us, consume us and transform us in our worship of the Father as we express our love for Him.

Halal Praise Has Three Main Objectives:

    a.   To celebrate or boast on the name of the Lord.
    b.   To celebrate or boast of the Word of the Lord.
    c.   To celebrate or boast of His mighty deeds.

a. His Name

Psa 69:30 NASB

> *I will praise (halal) the name of God with song, and shall magnify Him with thanksgiving.*

Names are very significant to a Hebrew, as they reveal the nature and character of a person. One of the names of God is 'Yaweh' or 'I AM', also translated as Lord or Adonai. This is Gods memorial name, or personal name to all generations, (Exodus 3:14-15). As we saw earlier God is saying through this name; "I am the one who was and is and always will be. I am not only the creator of life, but I am life. I am everything you need for life." As we praise this name we are celebrating the awesome life we see in God which has now become my life and your life. We are celebrating the fact that our God can do all things and be all things to us. His life is now our life! This is why I praise (halal) the Lord.

Throughout the Bible we find many names of God which reveal a particular aspect of His character and nature and which we may include in our worship experience. A good exercise would be to do a study on all of Gods names and His attributes and include these in your worship experience. Please see the Appendix for a listing of some of these names.

Q5. List some of the names of God which you would like to include in your worship experience.

_____

b. His Word

Col 3:16 NASB

> *Let the word of Christ richly dwell within you, with all wisdom teaching and admonishing one another with psalms and hymns and spiritual songs, singing with thankfulness in your hearts to God.*

Psa 56:4 NASB

> *In God, whose word I praise (halal), In God I have put my trust; I shall not be afraid. What can mere man do to me?*

We praise (halal) His word as God has spoken to us and revealed Himself to us. God has not kept silent nor rejected us, but has spoken and made known His will for our lives. This is good reason to celebrate! **I shall celebrate His Word because He has spoken and by His Word has revealed Himself to me.** I celebrate God's promises in His word and praise Him for them.

> Word = Dabar 1697 meaning speech, word.

So we praise (halal) Him for who He is and for His Word; He has revealed Himself and He has spoken with us. He is my life and with His voice He guides me and reveals all things to me. The word God speaks into my heart quickens me and I rejoice at hearing His voice. Halal is the manifestation of joy expressed through a heart filled with love, which His word has produced in us. If our hearts are filled with His word then our mouths will also be filled with praise for His word which He has revealed to me

c. His Deeds

Psa 150:2 NASB

> *Praise (halal) Him for His mighty deeds; Praise (halal) Him according to His excellent greatness.*

We celebrate and boast of His mighty deeds; the great things He has done for us. He sent His Son who died for our sins, who took upon Himself the judgement due each one of us. He has given us a new life, a new beginning. He has healed our minds and emotions, and given us hope and a destiny. He leads us each day by His Holy Spirit, and imparts His wisdom and knowledge into our hearts. We have a peace which is beyond comprehension and at times defies all logic. He causes all things to work out for our good, for those who love Him. The list is endless of what God has done for each one of us.

Q6. Make a list of the great things God has; done for you, made you to be, given you, set you free from, established in you,

_____

These lists should now become a foundation of your praise as you see what God has done for you and as you see who He is. Seek to continually expand these lists as it will enrich your worship experience.

Halal has three modes of expression

How do I celebrate His name, word and greatness? I celebrate;

- In song
- In dance
- With musical instruments.

2 Chr 29:30 NASB

Moreover, King Hezekiah and the officials ordered the Levites to sing praises (halal) to the LORD with the words of David and Asaph the seer. So they sang praises (halal) with joy, and bowed down and worshiped.

Psa 149:3 NASB

Let them praise (halal) His name with dancing; Let them sing praises to Him with timbrel and lyre.

Ezra 3:10 NASB

Now when the builders had laid the foundation of the temple of the LORD, the priests stood in their apparel with trumpets, and the Levites, the sons of Asaph, with cymbals, to praise (halal) the LORD according to the directions of King David of Israel.

Psa 69:30 NASB

I will praise (halal) the name of God with song, And shall magnify Him with thanksgiving.

Psa 150 NASB

Praise the LORD! Praise God in His sanctuary; Praise Him in His mighty expanse. Praise Him for His mighty deeds; Praise Him according to His excellent greatness. Praise Him with trumpet sound; Praise Him with harp and lyre. Praise Him with timbrel and dancing; Praise Him with stringed instruments and pipe. Praise Him with loud cymbals; Praise Him with resounding cymbals. Let everything that has breath praise the LORD. Praise the LORD!

We were created to be a creative people, after the image of God. Our worship must reflect this creativity in the way we worship our God. We are the expression of all God is; let us express it through the creative abilities we have been blessed with. **Let us sing, leap, dance and clap our hands in celebration to the Lord.**

It is as we see God in our lives every day that we are able to praise (halal) Him. This is a lifestyle of praise (halal), to see and experience God in your life every day and to celebrate and boast of your love for Him. Every day I should celebrate the blessing that God speaks to me and walks with me through all of life.

Application

Review all principles, questions and lists and spend some time in Halal (praise) to the Lord in light of what you have written down and discussed.

Make this a regular habit; let it be a part of your 'Lifestyle of Worship'

YADAH - 3034

Yadah praise is one in which we raise our hands in an outburst of spontaneous gratitude for what God has done. Our hands are used as an extension of our expression of thanks. One may also express thankful praise on a musical instrument.

Yadah: To throw, cast. Used in confession, praise and giving thanks.

Yadah means: To give thanks, laud or praise. An expression of thank or praise in ritual, public and personal praise. It is found mostly in the book of psalms, some 70 times.

Yadah comes from the root YAD meaning: hand. Yadah is to throw out the hands, or extend the hands in the giving of thanks as part of our worship experience.

Raising the hands is a symbol of acknowledgment that God alone has been the source of the blessing, He is the one who has brought about deliverance for us, and He is worthy of all praise. It is a universal symbol of jubilation in victory and one of surrender. It is praise given with a thankful heart for what God has done. It is the giving of thanks which one expresses through praise when deliverance has come, God has manifested Himself and we have seen and experienced the hand of God on our lives in some way. When we have tasted of His goodness and experienced His love in our lives then we must honour Him and give God thanks.

Principle: Yadah honours and acknowledges Gods hand and purpose over our lives. Yadah may be expressed vocally and with musical instruments. Our bodies become an extension of the expression of our hearts.

The following scriptures help to illustrate when we might give God praise (yadah). We find it touches every facet of life as God is continually blessing His people in a multitude of different ways.

Dan 2:23 NASB

"To Thee, O God of my fathers, I give thanks (yada) and praise, for Thou hast given me wisdom and power; Even now Thou hast made known to me what we requested of Thee, for Thou hast made known to us the king's matter."

Psa 138:4 NASB

All the kings of the earth will give thanks (yadah) to Thee, O LORD, when they have heard the words of Thy mouth.

Jer 33:11 NASB

the voice of joy and the voice of gladness, the voice of the bridegroom and the voice of the bride, the voice of those who say, "Give thanks (yadah) to the LORD of hosts, For the LORD is good, For His loving kindness is everlasting"; and of those who bring a thank offering into the house of the LORD. For I will restore the fortunes of the land as they were at first,' says the LORD.

Gen 29:35 NASB

And she conceived again and bore a son and said, "This time I will praise (yadah) the LORD." Therefore she named him Judah. Then she stopped bearing.

Psa 43:3-4 NASB

O send out Thy light and Thy truth, let them lead me; Let them bring me to Thy holy hill, And to Thy dwelling places. Then I will go to the altar of God, To God my exceeding joy; And upon the lyre I shall praise (yadah) Thee, O God, my God.

2Chr 7:3 NASB

And all the sons of Israel, seeing the fire come down and the glory of the LORD upon the house, bowed down on the pavement with their faces to the ground, and they worshiped and gave praise (yadah) to the LORD, saying, *"Truly He is good, truly His loving kindness is everlasting."*

Isa 12:4 NASB

And in that day you will say, "Give thanks (yadah) to the LORD, call on His name. Make known His deeds among the peoples; Make them remember that His name is exalted."

Q7. According to these scriptures why & when do we praise (Yadah) the Lord?

TOWDAH - 8426

Towdah is used in worship when coming before the Lord with a thank offering, or a sacrifice of thanksgiving. Towdah requires the release of faith as one is offering up thanksgiving for something God has not yet done, but which one believes God is about to do, or is able to do. It is thanking God for what He is about to do, even when circumstances may dictate otherwise. This type of faith will move mountains and open prison doors. When all seems lost and everything is against us, it will take a sacrifice to thank God in faith for deliverance.

Towdah comes from Yadah and means 'thanksgiving'.
Associated with sacrificing, was used of choirs or processions.

Towdah is used as: confession, hymns of thanksgiving, praise, sacrifice of thanksgiving, thank offering.

Principle: Towdah is a confession of faith that God is supreme and able to do all things.

This type of praise offered as a sacrifice means we will not consider our circumstances with our natural eyes, but we look only through the eyes of faith at our God our deliverer. Towdah is not to be underestimated as it will move the hand of God upon our lives.

A story is told of a pastor who once visited a critically ill child in hospital to pray for her, doctors held out little hope for this child. Instead of the pastor praying he stood by the bed, and lifting his hands he began to praise and thank God for healing this young child. He then left the hospital. He later received word that the child had made a miraculous recovery and was well.

Thanksgiving offered in faith is very powerful!

Psa 95:1 NASB

> *O come, let us sing for joy to the LORD; Let us shout joyfully to the rock of our salvation. Let us come before His presence with thanksgiving (towdah); Let us shout joyfully to Him with psalms.*

Psa 100:4 NASB

> *Enter His gates with thanksgiving (towdah), and His courts with praise. Give thanks to Him; bless His name. For the LORD is good; His loving kindness is everlasting, And His faithfulness to all generations.*

Psa 50:23 NASB

> *"He who offers a sacrifice of thanksgiving (towdah) honours Me; And to him who orders his way aright I shall show the salvation of God."*

Jonah 2:9-10 NASB

> *But I will sacrifice to Thee With the voice of thanksgiving (towdah). That which I have vowed I will pay. Salvation is from the LORD." Then the LORD commanded the fish, and it vomited Jonah up onto the dry land.*

Psa 116:17 NASB

> *To Thee I shall offer a sacrifice of thanksgiving (towdah), and call upon the name of the LORD.*

Psa 147:7 NASB

> *Sing to the LORD with thanksgiving (towdah); Sing praises to our God on the lyre,*

Q8. According to these scriptures why and when should we offer praise in thanksgiving (Towdah)?

We should always come into the presence of our heavenly Father with praises and with thanksgiving, even if it is as a sacrifice. The Christian walk is one of a continual sacrifice of one's life. We no longer walk according to this natural world we live in, but we walk according to the ways of the Spirit. We are now the sons and daughters of the living God, and we have been restored to His wonderful image, we now walk according to the image of Christ (Rom 8:29). Therefore when I come before the Father I thank Him for who I am in Christ by faith, I no longer see myself as the old sinful man but as a new man in Christ Jesus, full of His faith, love, hope, joy, power and authority, filled to overflowing with His Spirit. We no longer walk according to the flesh but according to the Spirit. It is a sacrifice because although we may not yet see the full manifestation of His promises in our lives, we live as though we have them, we walk in the Spirit. It is appropriate to thank Him for who we are today in Christ.

SHABACH – 7623B

As we see His loving kindness made manifest in our midst by His power to save, we can have only one response; it can only be one of shouting with joy in praise at what God has done for us. He has manifested His glorious power and delivered us.

Shabach means: to laud, praise.
It is used to commend, give glory, laud, and praise.

Psa 63:2-4 NASB

> *Thus I have beheld Thee in the sanctuary, To see Thy power and Thy glory. Because Thy loving kindness is better than life, My lips will praise (shabach) Thee. So I will bless Thee as long as I live; I will lift up my hands in Thy name.*

Psa 117:1-2 NASB

Praise (halal) the LORD, all nations; Laud (shabach) Him, all peoples! For His loving kindness is great toward us, and the truth of the LORD is everlasting. Praise (halal) the LORD!

1Chr 16:34-35 NASB

O give thanks to the LORD, for He is good; For His loving kindness is everlasting. Then say, "Save us, O God of our salvation, and gather us and deliver us from the nations, to give thanks to Thy holy name, And glory (shabach) in Thy praise."

Principle: Shabach is our response to seeing the manifestation of Gods power and glory towards us.

JOURNAL

The following is what I felt God speak to me concerning Shabach as I prayed for revelation.

Shabach is a shout of victory giving Me glory for what has occurred. When you see My hand move a mountain before you, you will praise Me, your heart will rejoice at what it sees and give a shout of confirmation that "My hand has done this!" Together as we walk as one you will see Me do great and mighty things in your midst, it is your hearts response as it leaps within to what it sees before you, My hand made manifest. Shout son; declare it to all that I am God!

Shabach is a declaration and shout of praise to all that we have seen; the glory of the Lord our God, and He has delivered by His mighty hand. We must be prepared to shabach the Lord before His people and before the nations declaring boastfully of God as our deliverer.

ZAMAR - 2167

Zamar means: To make music (in praise to God)
It is a song sung to the accompaniment of musical instruments.

Psa 47:6-8 NASB

Sing praises (zamar) to God, sing praises (zamar); Sing praises (zamar) to our King, sing praises (zamar). For God is the King of all the earth; Sing praises (zamar) with a skilful psalm. God reigns over the nations, God sits on His holy throne.

Psa 68:4,32 NAS)

Sing to God, sing praises (zamar) to His name; Lift up a song for Him who rides through the deserts, Whose name is the LORD, and exult before Him. Sing to God, O kingdoms of the earth; Sing praises (zamar) to the Lord, Selah.

Psa 71:22-23 NASB

> *I will also praise Thee with a harp, Even Thy truth, O my God; To Thee I will sing praises (zamar) with the lyre, O Thou Holy One of Israel. My lips will shout for joy when I sing praises (zamar) to Thee; And my soul, which Thou hast redeemed.*

Psa 144:9 NASB

> *I will sing a new song to Thee, O God; Upon a harp of ten strings I will sing praises (zamar) to Thee,*

Psa 149:3 NASB

> *Let them praise His name with dancing; Let them sing praises (zamar) to Him with timbrel and lyre.*

> Principle: Zamar is musical praise in song, its putting words to music in praise to God using a variety of instruments.

The greatest instrument is the heart, with musical instruments being an extension of the heart and giving expression to the heart of man. It is the singing of a spontaneous song from the heart as God gives us the melody. As Christians we are to be led by the Spirit in all things, this would include our worship and praise. Ask the Holy Spirit for a new song and you will find a song and melody bubbling up from within you.

Music is an extremely powerful way of stirring our emotions and expressing our emotions. Through music one can touch the very inner most part of a person's being for both good and evil. The instruments themselves are not evil, but they may draw out the evil in a person as music becomes an extension of one's soul expression. A musical instrument may be used in time of war to call an army to battle formation; stirring up man's heart for battle. It may also be used to restore peace to one whose heart is troubled. Under the anointing and leading of the Holy Spirit, music will open the heart of the believer to God in worship and take one into an intimate experience with God.

Conversely music played under satanic influence will open the door to demonic activity among those involved. This can be seen in places like Africa where ancestral worship is practiced; often those participating in the musical ritual will enter a trance like state as they become possessed by demons.

Music becomes an extension of who we are, expressing whatever is within our hearts. Since we are to be the expression of all that God is, music too may be an expression of the heart of God through us, stirring and drawing the Christian into a divine worship experience with the Father.

It is God within us providing the melody with which we sing words of praise. We are encouraged to 'sing a new song' that is one which bubbles up in our spirit, making melody with our hearts (Eph 5:19). Do not wait for Sunday to sing your praises to God, but sing a new song every day from your heart.

Music in churches is absolutely scriptural and the playing of all kinds of instruments should be encouraged. King David had literally thousands of musicians playing all kinds of instruments, many of which David himself made.

1 Chr 23:3-5 NASB

> *And the Levites were numbered from thirty years old and upward, and their number by census of men was 38,000. Of these, 24,000 were to oversee the work of the house of the LORD; and 6,000 were officers and judges, and 4,000 were gatekeepers, and 4,000 were praising the LORD with the instruments which David made for giving praise.*

TEHILLAH - 8416

Tehillah means: "glory; praise; song of praise; praiseworthy deeds."

Isa 60:18 NASB

> *"Violence will not be heard again in your land, Nor devastation or destruction within your borders; But you will call your walls salvation, and your gates praise (tehillah).*

Isa 61:1 NASB

> *The Spirit of the Lord GOD is upon me, Because the LORD has anointed me To bring good news to the afflicted; He has sent me to bind up the broken-hearted, To proclaim liberty to captives, And freedom to prisoners;*

Isa 61:3 NASB

> *To grant those who mourn in Zion, Giving them a garland instead of ashes, The oil of gladness instead of mourning, The mantle of* **praise** *(tehillah) instead of a spirit of fainting. So they will be called oaks of righteousness, The planting of the LORD, that He may be glorified.*

Isaiah likens Tehillah praise to a mantle and our lives as the walls and gates of a city, whose gates is our Tehillah praise. Let us consider each one of these separately.

Gate.

The wall in our lives is our salvation, with the Lord being our fortress. Within the walls of salvation dwells God in all His glory and splendour.

[1]The gates in ancient times were the only way in and out of a walled city. As gateways they had huge open spaces and were used as a public meeting place. They were like huge vaulted halls providing relief on a hot day.

The city gate was used as the public gathering place for the issuing of a public proclamation or address. It was also the place where an open court was held in the matters of justice. As such the gate of a city was viewed as a prominent meeting place; it became the place where the voice of the city could be expressed.

> Isaiah is saying that God dwells within us in all His glory, and our lives become the gateway or expression of His glory to the world. To offer Tehillah praise is to open my life up to reveal the glory of God within me. A life of holiness will proclaim His glory and give praise to God.

Mantle2

This was a large cloak worn as an outer garment by a Palestinian which would correspond to a Westerner's overcoat today. It was made of wool, goat's hair or sometimes cotton, and provided all year round protection from the heat and cold. Because of its size and the way it covered the whole body, it was also used as a means of carrying various things such as barley, (Ruth 3:15).

The picture we have then is of a multipurpose garment which was able to cover the entire body, providing protection from the weather and assisting the wearer in carrying various objects. It may have also become the most distinguishing feature of a person. This then was considered to be the most important single piece of garment the wearer possessed.

> Isaiah describes our tehillah praise as a mantle, as something valuable and precious which we wear and which covers our entire being. It gives us shelter from life and becomes the distinguishing mark upon our lives. It becomes a reflection of who we are; the expression of the glory of God, the revelation of His holiness in our lives and giving praise to God.

JOURNAL ON TEHILLAH PRAISE

The following is a question I asked the Lord about Tehillah praise.

"Lord what would you say to me about 'Tehillah' praise, what is it Lord?"

> My praise shall be exalted in My people. My people have been called by My name, they bear My name. I have given them My Spirit by which they can do all things. It is My name in their hearts which causes praise to go forth into all the world. I have given My name to empower and release My people. My name releases the captive and sets him free. Tehillah exalts Me as

---

[1]   Manners and Customs of Bible Lands. Fred Wight.

[2]   Manners and Customs of Bible Lands. Fred Wight.

it reveals My glory upon a person, it manifests My glory and name for all to see. Tehillah son is the highest honour I can be given. It reinforces My will and testimony in people's lives, it reveals My kingdom and brings it glory. It testifies to My goodness in people's hearts, as they know Me so they shall reflect Me in their lives. This honours Me son, to manifest My glory through you is the highest honour you bestow on Me. To sing My praises and acknowledge My presence and to give Me honour in all things. Tehillah is the expression of My glory in you to a world which cannot see Me. To give Me tehillah praise is to open your heart and allow My light to shine in you to a dying world. You are the testimony of My love, through you shall I reveal My glory. A lifestyle of Tehillah brings Me much glory as it testifies of all I am.

So Lord, when do I offer Tehillah praise to you?

Everyday son when you awake, you awake with My glory in you. It is as you open your heart that I manifest myself to you and through you. Tehillah is a life of revealing My glory in you, that gives me the highest praise.

Thankyou Lord.

If you will remember I said earlier on that we are to be the expression of all God is. Tehillah is my life in praise, it is not only the words I speak or sing in praise but also my very lifestyle gives God praise and brings Him glory and honour.

To know His name is to know God intimately; to have a close living and abiding relationship with Him, to have the presence of God. His name sets me free and by His Spirit I am empowered to live my life in His glorious image. The life I live testifies to the reality, goodness and power of God. We give God the highest honour by being a reflection or image of all that He is, in being the expression of His glory. Our Tehillah will radiate His glory and presence.

Tehillah can be better understood by the words of Jesus, He said we are the light of the world and should let our light shine before men, that they might give glory to God.

Mat 5:14-16 NASB

> *"You are the light of the world. A city set on a hill cannot be hidden. "Nor do men light a lamp, and put it under the peck-measure, but on the lamp stand; and it gives light to all who are in the house." Let your light shine before men in such a way that they may see your good works, and glorify your Father who is in heaven.*

This is Tehillah praise; to let your light shine, to let the glory of God shine out through you and be seen by all!

We are now the new tabernacles of God and the temple of the Holy Spirit. God dwells in us; He lives in us and expresses Himself through us.

Eph 2:22 NASB

in whom you also are being built together into a dwelling of God in the Spirit.

1Cor 3:16 NASB

Do you not know that you are a temple of God, and that the Spirit of God dwells in you?

John 17:22-23 NASB

"And the glory which Thou hast given Me I have given to them; that they may be one, just as We are one; I in them, and Thou in Me, that they may be perfected in unity, that the world may know that Thou didst send Me, and didst love them, even as Thou didst love Me.

Q9. Consider what these scriptures mean for your life?
What does it mean for you to be one in Spirit with God?

_____

We are also one in spirit with God, as I sense my spirit so I am touching God and sensing and experiencing the movement of God within me. As I release this movement of God within me into my life so I will bring praise and glory (tehillah) to God.

Principle: Tehillah is God in me, made manifest through my life, displaying His nature and character in the image and power of His son, bringing Him glory and praise.

Jesus said "From your innermost being shall flow rivers of living waters" referring to the flow of the Holy Spirit within us (Jn 7:38). The flow of the Spirit in our lives will reveal and manifest the glory of God to this world. This speaks of our walk in the Spirit, which as we manifest the fruit of the Spirit will bring glory (Tehillah) to God.

As Jesus went about His ministry healing and doing good (Ac 10:38), the people rejoiced in God and gave Him praise (Ac 3:8).

It is important to see that the very lives we live can radiate His glory and bring praise to God. Let us live our lives in such a way that man will see God in us and rejoice and give Him glory and praise.

Psa 106:1-2 NASB

Praise (tehillah) the LORD! Oh give thanks to the LORD, for He is good; For His loving kindness is everlasting. Who can speak of the mighty deeds of the LORD, Or can show forth all His praise? (tehillah).

Remember 'Tehillah' is the highest honour we can bestow on the Lord.

Every word I speak shall bring honour to the Lords name. This means every conversation, every discussion I have with anyone is to honour the Lord and His name. Let us be slow to speak and quick to praise our God.

Psa 34:1 NASB

(A Psalm of David when he feigned madness before Abimelech, who drove him) (away and he departed.) I will bless the LORD at all times; His praise (tehillah) shall continually be in my mouth.

Psa 71:8 NASB

My mouth is filled with Thy praise (tehillah), And with Thy glory all day long.

I will sing a new song; a song of the spirit, a song the Holy Spirit quickens to me revealing and glorifying God. It ceases to be my praise but it becomes the Holy Spirit praising God through me and bringing Him glory, touching the hearts of the unbeliever around me. Every word I speak shall release life and blessing that I might bring only glory to God.

Psa 40:3 NASB

And He put a new song in my mouth, a song of praise (tehillah) to our God; Many will see and fear, And will trust in the LORD.

Enter His Presence with Tehillah Praise

Psa 100:4 NASB

Enter His gates with thanksgiving, And His courts with praise (tehillah). Give thanks to Him; bless His name.

Whenever we come before the Lord it must be with thanksgiving and praise (Tehillah).

This means we come clothed with and radiating His glory and holiness in our lives. We come clothed in righteousness, not sin consciousness, we come displaying the new man in Christ, full of faith, full of the Life of Christ. As His children we are now filled with the Life of God and we now walk in His glorious image and likeness, this is how we stand before God and offer Him Tehillah praise! I see myself only according to His image and by the power of the Spirit I walk in His image. Our praise becomes a lifestyle, it is who we are

Q10. Is this how you see yourself each day? Is this how you present yourself to your Father? Spend some time meditating on what it means to have been created in His image & likeness and make a list of how you see yourself in His image.

BARAK - 1288

Barak means: to kneel, bless, be blessed, and curse.

God is the one who has first blessed us.

Gen 1:27-28 NASB

And God created man in His own image, in the image of God He created him; male and female He created them. And God blessed (barak) them; and God said to them, "Be fruitful and multiply, and fill the earth, and subdue it; and rule over the fish of the sea and over the birds of the sky, and over every living thing that moves on the earth."

God has given to man every good thing, every perfect gift from above, He has ministered to man; spirit, soul and body. We are also called upon to bless the Lord.

Psa 103:1,2 NASB (A Psalm of David.)

Bless the LORD, O my soul; and all that is within me, bless His holy name. Bless the LORD, O my soul, and forget none of His benefits;

The only way we can bless the Lord is by ministering to Him with our praises and our worship; we have nothing with which we could minister to God with, except with that which He has given us. If we are to bless the Lord with all that is within us then our lives and all we are must be a blessing to God. We can bless Him by using His gifts to bring glory to His name. My heart, my mind, my soul are all His for Him to use for His glory.

Combination of Praise Expressions

In Psalm 71 we can see three different expressions of praise within one psalm showing us the variety of ways with which we can praise God.

Psa 71:8 NASB

My mouth is filled with Thy praise (tehillah), And with Thy glory all day long.

Psa 71:14 NASB

But as for me, I will hope continually, And will praise (tehillah) Thee yet more and more.

Psa 71:15 NASB

My mouth shall tell of Thy righteousness, And of Thy salvation all day long; For I do not know the sum of them.

Psa 71:22 NASB

I will also praise (yadah) Thee with a harp, Even Thy truth, O my God; To Thee I will sing praises (zamar) with the lyre, O Thou Holy One of Israel.

Psa 71:23 NASB

My lips will shout for joy when I sing praises (zamar) to Thee; And my soul, which Thou hast redeemed.

Summary

Praise is the expression of the love I have for God and may be expressed in a multitude of different ways using everything I am and all I have; my voice, my song, my hands and feet and all kinds of musical instruments. I am limited only by my creativity and willingness to express myself and allow God to use me in my expression.

Praise will set us free emotionally to be what God wants us to be, our praises become a blessing not only to God but to ourselves, as God manifests Himself in our lives through our praises.

Let us not shrink back from praise, but putting aside all self-consciousness, let us praise the lover of our souls and minister to Him in our worship on a daily basis as a lifestyle, not waiting for Sunday but seeing everyday as a new opportunity to exalt our God.

Recap: What Principles have we learnt about the variety of Praise?

- "I am the expression of all God is!"
- If we are to be the expression of all God is, then our praise must also express and declare all God is.
- Praise becomes the overflow of what I have seen and experienced in God and cannot be contained. My heart attitude is one of love, gratitude and awe in His presence.
- Praise is the perfect response to all that God is within me as He reveals Himself to me.
- In Halal praise one ceases to be self-conscious of what others might think of our behaviour, being totally consumed by the passion of expressing our love for God. Halal is not what we express but how we express it; with joyous uninhibited celebration.
- Never be ashamed of openly expressing your love for God.
- The Word & Revelation become the basis of our praise.
- Yadah honours and acknowledges Gods hand and purpose over our lives. Yadah may be expressed vocally and with musical instruments. Our bodies become an extension of the expression of our hearts.
- Towdah is a confession of faith that God is supreme and able to do all things.
- Shabach is our response to seeing the manifestation of Gods power and glory towards us.
- Zamar is musical praise in song, its putting words to music in praise to God using a variety of instruments.

- Tehillah is God in me, made manifest through my life, displaying His nature and character in the image and power of His son, bringing Him glory and praise.

Assignment

1. Over the next two weeks spend some time everyday praising God by taking a different praise word each day and praising God accordingly. Praise Him at home, praise Him at work, praise Him in church, and praise Him anywhere you can.
2. Write either a poem or song expressing your love to the Lord.

CHAPTER SIX

The Lifestyle of Worship

"God is spirit, and those who worship Him must worship in spirit and truth." John 4:24

In this chapter we will be taking a further look at the principles of worship as a lifestyle and build upon our first lesson. God's heart cry today is for intimacy, He longs for an intimate relationship based on close fellowship. Our heavenly Father desires to reveal His heart and innermost feelings of love for us that we may experience His presence in our lives every day. Without worship we will never be able to achieve this, as praise expresses my heart in faith and draws me into His presence, worship allows me to enter into His rest; it is a place of peace and joy in the Holy Spirit. It is that place of intimacy where God will share His innermost thoughts with me, and where we can share the love we have together while I am sitting on His lap, with His arms wrapped around me. He is my Father and I am His child. An open heart is what the Father is looking for that He may speak into our lives daily.

A worshipper is one who will honour God with his life in all he does and all he is, while expressing his love unashamedly. He will give God the place of receiving the highest honour in his life by submitting his all to God as his sovereign Lord.

Jesus our Worship Leader

Jesus is to be Lord in every area of our lives and this includes worship. He is 'The Lion of the Tribe of Judah.' Judah means praise, and as a tribe they were stationed immediately opposite the entrance to the tabernacle of Moses. Symbolically Judah led Israel in their worship. Today Jesus joins us in praising the Father and leads us in our worship; let us follow His example which He taught us.

Rev 5:5 NASB

> *and one of the elders said^ to me, "Stop weeping; behold, the Lion that is from the tribe of Judah, the Root of David, has overcome so as to open the book and its seven seals."*

Psa 22:22 NASB

> *I will tell of Thy name to my brethren; In the midst of the assembly I will praise Thee.*

While on earth Jesus taught us how to pray, in the first line of His prayer (Matt 6:9-10) He says;

> 'Our Father who art in heaven, Hallowed be Thy name. 'Thy kingdom come. Thy will be done, On earth as it is in heaven.'

The New Testament opens with Jesus presenting God as our Father, no longer do we only serve Him as God but we now know Him as Father. The unsaved world knows Him as God, but we who have been redeemed by the precious blood of Jesus know Him as Father. Why? We are not far away, but have now been brought near to the Father, by the blood of Christ (Eph 2:13). Man in Old Testament times could only gaze from a distance but now we can stand in His very presence and see Him in all His glory.

Father implies lineage and intimacy. Whereas before, my lineage went back to the 'father of lies' the devil who gave us our corrupt sinful nature, today our lineage goes back once again to 'The Father of Life', who has birthed His own holy nature within us. He is my Father because I now carry His

DNA in me which is the Spirit and the image of Christ. The Fathers DNA is in the Son, and the sons DNA is now in us, we are all one through the DNA; we are to be holy as the Father is holy. So God is now my Father!

"Hallowed be thy name." In other words "I will reverence your name and give you all honour in my life. I will open my heart to you and receive your voice in your presence, and listen to every word you will speak to me, that my life may be a channel for you to bless and manifest your presence in this world."

This is the essence of worship. Jesus taught us to see God as our Father and how to worship Him.

Q1. Jesus saw God as His Father and always spoke of God as His Father. How do you see and speak of God in your life?

The Role of the Holy Spirit in Worship

Jesus has cleared the way and leads us into the Fathers presence, and the Holy Spirit is the one who empowers us to worship, He is the one who enlightens the eyes of our hearts to see the Father and gives us revelation of the Father. He is the one who gives us the song to sing as we see the Father.

Eph 5:18 NASB

> *And do not get drunk with wine, for that is dissipation, but be filled with the Spirit, speaking to one another in psalms and hymns and spiritual songs, singing and making melody with your heart to the Lord; always giving thanks for all things in the name of our Lord Jesus Christ to God, even the Father;*

When next you praise the Father ask the Holy Spirit to give you a new song to sing to the Father.

Worship is what will open the door to intimacy in our Lives.

The Father longs for intimacy with His children, just as He walked with and knew Adam & Eve so He longs to walk with and know you and I. Christ has made the way for us, now worship is the catalyst for intimate fellowship with the Father.

The following is a journal I wrote when I asked the Lord about His thoughts on worship in my life. They reveal the heart of the Father and His greatest desire for us; the sharing of life together.

Journal

Lord how do you see the area of praise and **worship** being integrated into life on a daily basis?

It is not a work son, but just being with Me will produce the results you seek. To know Me is to have life, as I give life to those who seek Me. Son when you come before Me and honour My name, I open My heart to you to know Me. I give you your desires each day. Your worship son opens your heart that I might bless you. This is not something you do, but something you become, you begin to live your life with a continual open heart before Me, this is called abiding, as you abide so I am able to bless you every day. Abiding is My Spirit entwined with yours and being one. Worship opens the door to living your life as one with Me. It is not an act but a way of life.

Thankyou Lord.

From the above journal the Lord is saying:

If you will love and honour me by continually opening your heart up to Me, then I will open My heart up to you and bless you daily as we abide and live together as one in spirit.

This is the key to living and experiencing the abundant life Jesus promised in John 10:10. Consider the following scriptures in light of your fellowship with the Father.

John 15:5,7-8 NASB

*"I am the vine, you are the branches; he who **abides** in Me, and I in him, he bears much fruit; for apart from Me you can do nothing." If you abide in Me, and My words abide in you, ask whatever you wish, and it shall be done for you. "By this is My Father glorified, that you bear much fruit, and so prove to be My disciples.*

John 17:22-23 NASB

*"And the glory which Thou hast given Me I have given to them; **that they may be one, just as We are one**; I in them, and Thou in Me, that they may be perfected in unity, that the world may know that Thou didst send Me, and didst love them, even as Thou didst love Me.*

Jesus first called on the disciples to follow Him (Matt 4:19), He later gave the instruction that we are to **abide** in Him.

Q2. Discuss what 'abiding' and 'being one' means to a worshipper.

_____

Q3. Discuss the difference between following and abiding.

Love – The Catalyst to Worship

1 Tim 1:5 NASB

> *But the goal of our instruction is **love from a pure heart** and a good conscience and a sincere faith.*

[3]It is said that our spirit can be defined as our underlying:

- Motives
- Attitudes
- Character traits

Whilst submission to God as our Father may be our attitude in worship, love is what motivates us to honour Him as our Father. Love should be our only motive in worshipping our Father, and never what I can get from God, in fact love for our Father should be the only motivator in anything we do in life, anything short of this and we are simply producing a dead work. Love from a pure heart is unselfish and does not seek its own.

In worship I have entered into Gods rest, I am no longer striving with faith, but I am resting in His presence and I am just simply loving and being loved by My Father.

Consider what Psalm 46 has to say about striving. Please read and note especially what verse ten has to say about striving.

Q4. Discuss why vs10 is important in a loving and abiding relationship with the Lord.

The Distinguishing Elements of Praise & Worship

The following two illustrations will help to highlight the difference between praise and worship; the first illustration takes a look at praise.

> I saw the Father in the distance and I began to shout my praises to Him as I ran towards Him with joy inexpressible in my heart, until I found myself face to face with My Father. Then I was in awe of Him and just stood there soaking up His love and presence, quietly telling Him how much I loved Him and pouring out my heart to Him. He took me by the hand and sat me on His knee, there was a big smile on His face and His eyes twinkled with delight and radiated His love for me. Then He whispered "I know my child, but rest in Me now, let me wipe away your tears and I will tell you what I have planned for your life, I will show you what

---

[3] Abiding in Christ by Mark & Patti Virkler

I will do for you for I love you so much. I will never leave you but I am always with you. When you trip and fall I am there, when you celebrate a victory I am there, because you see My child I am with you and in you to live life with you forever." I felt His strength, experienced His love and I began to see my Father in a way I had never seen Him before. I was glad we had spent this time together, for now my love for my Father was ever deeper than before. I realised that in His presence I can rest in His arms and He will refresh me always. I can come to Him with all my troubles and He will always show me His ways and lead me to victory.

Praise takes me into His presence, whereas in worship I am resting in and experiencing the Fathers love in my heart. The next illustration highlights Worship.

When the whistle blew the train left the station; 'Faith' was the name of the engine pulling the carriages along on their way; their destination was 'worship'. On their way Faith caught many glimpses of 'Worship', their destination, every time Faith saw Worship he blew his whistle and gave off a mighty shabach, all the while the rumbling carriage wheels sang a halal with towdah; they were on their way to meet with 'Worship'. When the train finally arrived at their destination 'Worship' was waiting for them. The train stopped, Faith had done its work, shabach and halal had alerted 'Worship' who was ready and waiting for the Prince. 'Worship' immediately took the Prince into the Kings presence where he was received and given a royal welcome; for you see the King loved the Prince with such a great love. They sat down and had a wonderful time of fellowship together, their eyes betraying the love they had for each other. At the end of the day when they said their farewells, the King brought out His precious gifts for the Prince to take back with Him, so many gifts in fact that the train was very quickly filled to overflowing and could take no more. The King then placed His signet ring on the Princes finger and said, "With this ring I will be with you where-ever you go." And so the Prince returned to his home, all the while the train's engine; 'Faith' was blowing his whistle in yadah and the wheels sang a zamar love song to the King.

Q5. Describe how praise differed to worship in the above illustration.

The Greek Definition of Worship

As with praise, we also have a number of different words to describe worship, one being the Greek word, proskuneo.

Proskuneo means: to do reverence to.
It is translated as: - bow down, worship, prostrate.

Proskuneo is derived from two Greek words; Pros and Kuneo

Pros denote motion from a place, towards or at a place.
Kuneo means to kiss.

John 4:24 NASB

> *"God is spirit, and those who worship (proskuneo) Him must worship (proskuneo) in spirit and truth."*

From the above we can see proskuneo is a movement towards another with the intention to kiss.

> Principle: Proskuneo implies worship based on an intimate relationship in which love is the primary motivation.

God is love and it was with love that He first moved towards us to redeem us and restore us to the intimate relationship we once enjoyed in the Garden of Eden. Our response too is one of love as we move towards our Father giving Him honour for who He is.

During my childhood years while I was growing up, I had a great admiration and love for my father; he meant the world to me. I looked up to him for everything, he was my mentor, my teacher, my protector and I honoured my father by being obedient to him not because I had to, but because I loved him and wanted only to please him in whatever way I could. I looked up to him and respected him for who he was, a loving father who cared for his family. Quite often people would comment on how much I was like my father, not only in looks, but also in character. When we are in a loving relationship we tend to begin to blend in and become one in our thoughts, words and deeds. A father becomes a child's role model, and the child learns to do and say the things it sees in its father.

This is what our Father is looking for in our worship, a relationship based on love and honour. This is what proskuneo looks like; I love and look up to my heavenly Father seeking only to do His will in my life that I might honour His Name in all that I do. I love to spend time in His presence as I lay my heart bare before Him while expressing my heart and waiting upon Him, so that He may speak into my life and flow through me by His Spirit. As I do so I begin to display more and more of my Fathers character and nature as we become one.

Proskuneo is a Father Son relationship, not a master servant relationship. Worship is the greatest blessings which God has given us, as through worship He is able to give us so much of Himself. Worship gives God the opportunity to bless us abundantly above and beyond what we can think or imagine.

Worship is for our benefit as it gives us the opportunity to bless and be blessed. We have the unique ability to minister to the heart of our Father and bless Him and in doing so as we minister to His heart, He opens up the flood gates of heaven and blesses our lives. God first loved us and gave His son, as we respond with love so God also responds to our love and pours out His blessings upon our lives.

Worship from a heart filled with love is the key which opens the door to intimacy and great blessings. In worship we may bow our knees but more importantly we bow our hearts, being transparent before the Father and motivated only by our love for our Father.

Worship – My life of Service

Worship is not about the type of song I sing, or whether I sing a fast or slow song, worship is not in the singing but in the heart. Worship is not an act but a lifestyle; it is a lifestyle of living with a continual open heart to the Father, and submitted to the work of the Spirit in my life. Neither is worship something I do once a week when I attend church, but rather worship is a daily lifestyle which I bring into the church once a week.

We now have a second word for worship in the Greek:

Latreuo = a hired servant, to serve.

Phil 3:3 NASB

*for we are the true circumcision, who **worship (latreuo)** in the Spirit of God and glory in Christ Jesus and put no confidence in the flesh,*

Our service to God is considered a part of our worship to God, when it is according to the Spirit in our lives. We do not seek our own but we walk after the Spirit, doing only that which is on the Fathers heart for my life, doing His will. Restraint in our lives is as much an act of worship as is obedience.

Principle: Latreuo is the submission of my life to the leading of the Holy Spirit rather than the leading of my old sinful nature.

When man worships according to his old sinful nature he sets up idols in his life, but when my worship is according to the leading of the Spirit, then I worship in spirit and truth.

A spirit led life is one which honours God and brings Him glory. I am a worshipper (latreuo) when I live my life according to the leading of the Spirit and my worship (lifestyle) is acceptable to God. When I say I am a worshipper, I am saying that I am one submitted to the leading of the Holy Spirit for my life, and I honour the Holy Spirit in my life.

1Cor 14:15 NASB

What is the outcome then? I shall pray with the spirit and I shall pray with the mind also; I shall sing with the spirit and I shall sing with the mind also.

John 14:23 NASB

Jesus answered and said to him, "If anyone loves Me, he will keep My word; and My Father will love him, and We will come to him, and make Our abode with him.

Those who love God, worship (latreuo) Him by being submitted to the leading of the Holy Spirit; and who reveal truth by keeping His word.

Worship – A Lifestyle of Sacrifice

Rom 12:1 NASB

> *I urge you therefore, brethren, by the mercies of God, to **present your bodies a living and holy sacrifice,** acceptable to God, which is your **spiritual service of worship (Latreia).***

Latreia = Divine worship, service of worship.

Worship is a lifestyle of sacrifice. We daily offer our lives as a sacrifice to God, we are living sacrifices not dead ones. I am to present to God all that I am that He may flow His Spirit through me, so my life may become the expression of God in me, living a holy life.

> Principle: Latreia; I crucify the deeds of the flesh with its passions and desires and live by the fruit of the Spirit.

Please read Galatians 5:16-25.

This means I present all of my faculties to God for Him to flow through and use for His glory.

I would present my:

- Mind – I walk in revelation & anointed reasoning.
- Emotions - I walk with Gods heart, a heart of love and compassion not lust.
- Mouth – I speak the oracles of God as I hear God speak to me. I declare His praises. I speak only those things which edify seasoning my speech with grace.
- Eyes - I walk in the visions of God, doing only the things I see the Father doing, I live out of divine initiative. I use my eyes for the glory of God and not for the perversion of the flesh.
- Ears of my heart – I listen to the voice of God.
- Hands - I praise Him and allow Him to flow His healing power through my hands to heal others.
- Feet - I dance before the Lord as an expression of praise.

The apostle Paul says that my life is no longer my own, I have been bought with a price and it now belongs to the Holy Spirit to flow Gods anointing and life through me.

1Cor 6:19,20 NASB

> *Or do you not know that your body is a temple of the Holy Spirit who is in you, whom you have from God, and that you are not your own? For you have been bought with a price: therefore glorify God in your body.*

Paul also said that I am no longer living, I have died to my old sinful nature and it is now Christ living in me, it is now Christ in action in my life and it is no longer me in action in my life. This becomes a part of my lifestyle of worship; submitting my all to God that He may be all in all.

Gal 2:20 NASB

"I have been crucified with Christ; and it is no longer I who live, but Christ lives in me; and the life which I now live in the flesh I live by faith in the Son of God, who loved me, and delivered Himself up for me.

Q6. Describe in your own words a lifestyle of Latreuo & Latreia.

Worship – To bow down

Shachah means: To bow down.

This is a Hebrew word for worship indicating one would bow down before the Lord in worship or reverence to God.

In the context of the New Testament worship one may literally bow down or kneel before the Lord or submit to and open our hearts to the moving of the Holy Spirit in our lives as our worship to God.

Summary

To summarize worship as a lifestyle we have seen that worship is:

- The heart attitude of submission to and honouring God as our Father and expressing our intense love and profound respect we have for the Lord our God. It is an attitude which must in essence be expressed through our lives each and every day.
- My life becoming a platform for expressing my love for God and according to John 14:23 I am led by the Holy Spirit.
- A variety of expressions:
  1. Giving thanks for all God has done.
  2. Praising God in celebration, song, music, and dance, as an expression of my love and faith.
  3. I am the expression of all God is.
- Motivated by love.
- Submission of my life to the leading of the Holy Spirit rather than the leading of my old sinful nature.
- A lifestyle of sacrificing the flesh and presenting to God all that I am so He may flow His Spirit through me, that my life may be holy and become the expression of God in me.

The life of a worshipper may be aptly expressed by the following scripture:

Eph 5:18-21 NASB

And do not get drunk with wine, for that is dissipation, but be filled with the Spirit, speaking to one another in psalms and hymns and spiritual songs, singing and making melody with your heart to the Lord; always giving thanks for all things in the name of our Lord Jesus Christ to God, even the Father; and be subject to one another in the fear of Christ

Final Definition of a Lifestyle of Worship

To love God with a grateful heart while openly expressing my love and allowing intimacy with God to guide my life, as He births the things of His Spirit within me that I might be the expression of all that God is.

May this definition help to define your own life as a worshipper before the Lord our God, who is more than worthy of our praises. Having died for our sins and set us free from all condemnation, Jesus Christ the Son of God has opened the way into the presence of the Father, that we may be one in Spirit.

CHAPTER SEVEN

Psalms in Worship

Be filled with the Spirit, speaking to one another in psalms and hymns and spiritual songs

The book of Psalms has been a great source of inspiration to me over the years; the more I read it the more I noticed the heart of worship being demonstrated by King David and the other Psalmists. I discovered that worship for David was more than just telling God how much he loved him; instead it was a sharing of life together as David would often bring his life experiences into his worship. It was a sharing of love and life together.

David would frequently pour out his concerns with life and his frustrations with his fellow man, often being pursued by his enemies who sought to take his life. Yet through it all he would always give God the glory. David walked with God; he shared his heart with God and always put his final trust in Him, it was almost as if he and God were partners in life. His sharing became a part of his worship experience. He never took his eyes off His Lord despite the difficult times, but chose instead to worship his God through those experiences.

It is no wonder that God described David as 'a man after His own heart'. David is today an example for us of a true worshipper, one who knew how to worship in spirit and truth. One who delighted in His God and was unashamed in openly declaring his love for Him: the One whom He saw as more than creator of heaven and earth. He was the lover of his soul, the One who revealed himself as his counsellor and strength, the One who sustained him through all of life, the One on whom he could rely upon and trust with his very life. God and life were synonymous to David, you could not separate them. God was not someone you put on a mantel piece and acknowledge once a week, no he learnt to share life with God, and his praise in the psalms is a reflection of this.

We find psalms mentioned in the New Testament as well, it is almost as if God is saying "What I had with David I want to experience with you as well! I want to share life with you, the good the bad and the ugly, I want you to experience my love, my strength and wisdom flowing through your lives as it did through David, and then sing it and declare it to the world."

Col 3:16 NASB

> *Let the word of Christ richly dwell within you, with all wisdom teaching and admonishing one another with psalms and hymns and spiritual songs, singing with thankfulness in your hearts to God.*

Eph 5:18-20 NASB

> *And do not get drunk with wine, for that is dissipation, but be filled with the Spirit, speaking to one another in psalms and hymns and spiritual songs, singing and making melody with your heart to the Lord; always giving thanks for all things in the name of our Lord Jesus Christ to God, even the Father;*

The Apostle Paul on two occasions, with two different churches, emphasised 'psalms, hymns and spiritual songs', as being a natural part of our walk with God. Perhaps this is an area overlooked by many today in the church, simply because it is little understood. In this chapter we will examine the Psalms so you may gain a better appreciation for them, and see how they were used as a part of the life of King David and the other psalmists.

The Book of Psalms

God has given us the Psalms as His Praise manual to teach us how to praise His name and to show us that He desires to be a significant part of our lives. We have been created not only to know God but also to praise and worship God, and the Hebrew title of the book of Psalms makes this clear as it points to praise, while the Greek title points to music and poetry. They are therefore poems set to music, directing one to praise God. They are poetry sung as an expression of praise to God.

The psalms were written by people who knew God to be the Almighty Sovereign Lord, but who also lived in a troubled world. The psalms bring with them the reality of living in this world with all of its troubles and the experiences of trusting God through them all, and their responses. The psalms are a collection of mans' response to life and God. Sometimes they reveal man deeply grieved, doubting and in despair, and other times as very joyful and full of hope and faith. God used these experiences to magnify His name above every situation; these resulted in two types of psalms; Psalms of Lament, and Psalms of Praise.

Names of the Book

The Hebrew title for this book is Tehillim, meaning 'praises', which is the central theme for this book.

The Greeks translated the Hebrew word Mizmor, meaning 'song', as Psalmos which is frequently used as titles to individual psalms. The book was given the title Psalmoi (Psalms), from which we have the English translation of 'Psalms', which means 'sacred song sung to musical accompaniment'

Another English title comes from the Greek Septuagint, 'Psalterion' as 'Psalter'. Psalterion means 'Stringed instruments'.

Historical Background

The Book of Psalms is a collection of sacred poems, with many of them being in fact prayers. These poems were used as prayers and worship songs, and were sung in both private and public worship. Many of the psalms in fact would have been sung in the temple, while others were used in private worship and subsequently used in public worship.

The Book of Psalms was written over a period of several centuries as a book of 'common prayer' and although many of the psalms were sung, it was not considered a hymnal as we would consider hymnals today. They reflected the heart and faith of a nation as well as individuals such as King David, and as such could be considered as a guide for life. One can trace the life of David through the Psalms and become acquainted with his trials, tribulations, and victories. As we do so we too can receive comfort as we trace his footsteps. A good example would be Psalm 51, where we find David pouring his heart out to the Lord, and also Psalm 50, where David reveals God not only as our creator but also as the One who judges the heart of man. In response to David the Lord then speaks and addresses the nation of Israel and reproves their hardness of heart, showing them that He would prefer to see their worship coming from their hearts with thanksgiving and praise.

The Five Books

The Psalms were put together over a period of about one thousand years, from the time of Moses to the days of Ezra, and are made up of a collection of five books.

1. Book One Psalms 1 – 41
This book is about Man, his state of blessedness, fall and recovery. David probably wrote all the psalms in this book with the exception of Psalm One.
2. Book Two Psalms 42 – 72
This book is about Israel as a nation and their worship. It contains mostly Davidic Psalms except of the last one, Ps 72 which was written by Solomon.
3. Book Three Psalms 73 – 89
This book is about the Sanctuary, and how the life and worship of the nation revolved around the Sanctuary. Of the seventeen psalms in this book, eleven were written by Asaph, who was the chief musician in David's time and was involved in the sanctuary.
4. Book Four Psalms 90 - 106
This book is about the Earth, and includes the Royal Psalms (Ps 93 – 99). These psalms were written by a variety of authors. Ten were written by the sons of Korah (a guild of musical singers and composers).
5. Book Five Psalms 107 – 150
This book is about the Word and includes the Psalms of Ascents (Ps120 – 134). Again these were written by a variety of authors.

The psalms teach us that worship and praising God is what life is all about. Without praise there can be no meaningful life of faith, since it acknowledges God as our creator and the One who sustains our lives.

The Structure of Hebrew Poetry

Hebrew poetry is not structured around rhythm, but parallelism, whereas English poetry is characterized by repeated rhythms. The Australian Pocket Dictionary defines 'rhythm' in poetry as; 'the arrangement of words into a sequence of stressed and unstressed or long and short syllables.'

Parallelism is as a finely tuned musical instrument, in the hands of an accomplished musician, it becomes an extension of that person, and a medium which allows for the expression of the heart and the stirring of the emotions of the listener to worship.

Principle of Parallelism

Parallelism is the expression of a thought or statement in the first line as a form of introduction.

Great is the Lord God of heaven and earth!

This is followed by a second line which is an expansion on the first line of thought. It may express it differently or it may expound on that thought, drawing one ever deeper into the subject.

> He spoke and the heavens existed, He spoke and the worlds were created by the power of
> His might.
> Great is the Lord God of heaven and earth!
> Who has formed man from the dust and breathed His life into man.
> Who gives life in abundance and without measure.
> How great is the Lord!
> He has redeemed our souls and breathed His life afresh and filled us with
> His glory.
> How great is the Lord!

The subject in this example is the greatness of God, the Lord of heaven and earth. Whilst the second line tells us why God is great and why He is Lord. This has the effect of sustaining the focus on the subject as it is expanded upon. In so doing, it allows the mind and heart of the one praying to be opened up to further revelation and the expression of love and faith.

Here we begin to see the beauty of the psalms, as it takes us beyond the familiar 'Praise the Lord' in our worship, to a declaration of why we praise Him, why is He worthy of our praises? We begin to express our hearts to the Lord, in keeping with our initial definition of worship; the attitude of the heart expressed in the presence of God.

As I see God through the eyes of my heart, so I begin to declare it in praise. This blesses the Lord and we in turn are blessed as our faith is raised to new levels. I can also begin to draw on my life just as King David drew on his, and praise God for it.

There are two types of Parallelism. There is Synonymous Parallelism, and Antithetic Parallelism.

'Synonymous' means: 1. having the same meaning. 2. Closely associated with.

'Antithesis' means: 1. the exact opposite. 2. Rhetoric. The placing together of contrasting ideas or words to produce an effect of balance.

Synonymous Parallelism

Synonymous parallelism means that there is a flow of continuity of thought or expression from the first line which is carried forward into subsequent lines. These may not necessarily be the same but they do not contradict each other.

Psalm 41:1-3 gives us an example of synonymous parallelism.

> *How blessed is he who considers the helpless;*
> *The LORD WILL DELIVER HIM IN A DAY OF TROUBLE.*
> *The LORD WILL PROTECT HIM AND KEEP HIM ALIVE,*
> *And he shall be called blessed upon the earth;*
> *And do not give him over to the desire of his enemies.*
> *The LORD WILL SUSTAIN HIM UPON HIS SICKBED;*
> *In his illness, You restore him to health.*

The subject line of this psalm is the blessings which will come upon the one who will assist those in need. The following lines reveal how this will come about; they do not contradict but continue the flow of the subject.

The following example is one which may be typical of my life today.

> Lord you have truly blessed me today with a great day;
> For I have experienced your peace in difficult times,
> I have walked in your strength and accomplished the impossible,
> I have known your wisdom in discerning truth which has astounded many,
> Surely your blessings have overtaken me today.

Antithetic Parallelism

Antithetic parallelism is used to state the opposite of the subject line. It may introduce contrasting ideas, thoughts or expressions, allowing one to reflect on life from man's perspective and God's perspective.

Ps 5 is an example of antithetic parallelism; it is a psalm contrasting the righteous and the wicked.

Thesis

> *Give ear to my words, O Lord,*
> *Consider my groaning.*
> [2] *Heed the sound of my cry for help, my King and my God,*
> *For to You I pray.*
> [3] *In the morning, O Lord, You will hear my voice;*
> *In the morning I will order my prayer to You and eagerly watch.*

Antithesis

⁴ For You are not a God who takes pleasure in wickedness;
No evil dwells with You.
⁵ The boastful shall not stand before Your eyes;
You hate all who do iniquity.
⁶ You destroy those who speak falsehood;
The Lord abhors the man of bloodshed and deceit.

Thesis

⁷ But as for me, by Your abundant loving kindness I will enter Your house,
At Your holy temple I will bow in reverence for You.
⁸ O Lord, lead me in Your righteousness because of my foes;

Make Your way straight before me.

Antithesis

⁹ There is nothing reliable in what they say;
Their inward part is destruction itself.
Their throat is an open grave;
They flatter with their tongue.
¹⁰ Hold them guilty, O God;
By their own devices let them fall!
In the multitude of their transgressions thrust them out,
For they are rebellious against You.

Thesis

¹¹ But let all who take refuge in You be glad,
Let them ever sing for joy;
And may You shelter them,
That those who love Your name may exult in You.
¹² For it is You who blesses the righteous man, O Lord,
You surround him with favor as with a shield.

A personal application may be as follows:

Lord I thank you for your abundant grace toward me.
I stand today in your presence, clothed with your glory,
Filled with your life and righteousness.
So different is my life today because of You!
Before I knew you, I walked in sin and shame,
I was dead in my sins and did not know it.

I was far from you; my lips did not praise you.
I walked in my own understanding and wisdom.
But today we walk as one and I am filled to overflowing,
I walk in your strength and my heart is filled with a new song.
My lips shall praise you forever more.
So different is my life today because of You!

I believe these principles of parallelism should be integrated into our personal worship experience as they enrich our praises, release faith in our hearts and bring a renewed freedom of expression into our lives.

Types of Psalms

Broadly speaking the Book of Psalms is made up of psalms of Lament and Praise. The first three books are predominantly psalms of lament, while the last two books are predominantly psalms of praise. Despite this, praise is the central theme of the book and is to be found the whole way through the book. Despite the book being made up of approximately two thirds as psalms of lament, these psalms still move one toward praising God.

There are two basic types of praise psalms. There are the psalms which declare praise to God and then there are the psalms which describe God and His attributes.

The psalms which declare praise are the Hallal psalms, or Hallelujah psalms, where one is praising God without giving specific details of why or for what the psalmist is praising God.

The psalms describing God tell us why we should praise Him. A psalm may include both types with a noticeable transition from declaring to describing God. An example is Psalm 113, with the transition occurring in verse 5.

> *Praise the LORD!*
> *Praise, O servants of the LORD,*
> *Praise the name of the LORD.*
> *² Blessed be the name of the LORD*
> *From this time forth and forever.*
> *³ From the rising of the sun to its setting*
> *The name of the LORD IS TO BE PRAISED.*
> *⁴ The LORD IS HIGH ABOVE ALL NATIONS;*
> *His glory is above the heavens.*
> *⁵ Who is like the LORD OUR GOD,*
> *Who is enthroned on high,*
> *⁶ Who humbles Himself to behold*
> *The things that are in heaven and in the earth?*
> *⁷ He raises the poor from the dust*
> *And lifts the needy from the ash heap,*
> *⁸ To make them sit with princes,*

With the princes of His people.
⁹ He makes the barren woman abide in the house
As a joyful mother of children.
Praise the LORD!

It must be noted that not all psalms were written for temple worship. Some were written for temple worship while others were personal expressions of gratitude for God's mighty deeds and goodness, which may have been incorporated into temple worship at a later stage. The psalms were written for both public and private use.

Major Themes of the Psalms of Praise

We can find four major themes in the palms of praise. They are:

- Creation.
- The universal presence and sovereignty of God.
- Israel's history.
- God's awesome deeds.

Bringing creation into the psalms is one way of showing that the world belongs to God, which gives Him certain rights and privileges, since He ruled over kings and nations. One may think the major reason for praising God is for His protection, deliverance or for being a loving shepherd. However, the psalms of praise often point to creation, historical events, God's universal reign and mighty deeds.

The Psalms in Daily Life

King David's Psalms reveal his life experiences with his fellow man and God in the midst of it all, they are based on what was happening in his life and not on fantasy. His God was very real to him, and became a part of his life's experiences. Many of the psalms he wrote were actually his prayers and how God answered those prayers.

In the midst of life David knew His God and God became a part of his daily life. His praise expressed his heart towards God and He was never ashamed to praise Him. His praises were carved out of his faith in his God to overcome despite whatever life threw at him. He was never moved by life's situations, rather by what he knew His God could do in life's situations. This was his hallmark, his unshakeable faith in God which became the expression of his praises.

We too must endeavour to do the same as David; to know our God and express our hearts to him in praise in the midst of life's turmoils. We are to be real with our God and not play church, bring Him into our daily lives and give Him thanks in all things, praising Him in the midst of every situation.

It is as I praise Him that the might of His power will become real to me, as it focuses on what God is able to do and not on what I can do. This is the power of praise; it releases the faith of God within you for the impossible as He reveals Himself to you.

Principle: Praise God for His Name, Deeds and Word in your daily life.

Meditation the Key to Praise

Psa 1:1-2 NASB

How blessed is the man who does not walk in the counsel of the wicked, Nor stand in the path of sinners, Nor sit in the seat of scoffers! But his delight is in the law of the LORD, And in His law he meditates day and night.

It is of interest to note the very first psalm begins with the call to meditate on God and His Word. Why is this significant? It is as we meditate on God, and His word, that revelation and illumination begin to flow from the Holy Spirit, since meditation is both a heart and mind function. It is as I see with my heart that my mind comprehends and I begin to walk in unity with the Holy Spirit, causing faith to arise in my heart resulting in praise to the Father.

In Psalm 4:4 David acknowledges the power and significance of meditating on God, in fact he even encourages us to meditate when we are lying down. He is encouraging us to be still before the Lord and let God speak into our hearts.

Psa 4:4 NASB

Tremble, and do not sin; Meditate in your heart upon your bed, and be still. Selah.

It's as we meditate that God begins to open up His Word to us, and revelation of who His is flows and fills our hearts, so that we begin to see God for who He really is; a loving, almighty God, full of grace and truth. As our hearts fill with revelation, so too will our praises increase, as we see Him so we will praise Him with a new song in our hearts.

Life Application

As we saw at the beginning of this chapter, the apostle Paul encourages us to sing psalms, hymns and spiritual songs. When Paul spoke of Psalms I believe he was not only referring to the book of Psalms, but that we should speak our own psalms as well. Remember the Psalms were the Hebrew style of poetry used to praise the Lord. I believe it is important to understand this concept of praise and develop it as part of our own worship.

I personally found my praise life blossomed once I understood some of the fundamentals of the psalms, I found my worship experience grew as I applied these to all I had learnt of praise and thanksgiving. I also found it began to be a source of encouragement to others in my church, helping to open the hearts of God's people to receive the ministry of the Holy Spirit.

These principles have helped me tremendously in developing a lifestyle of worship, whereby it has become second nature for me to praise God in all things at all times, where ever I might be. It has brought me to a level of freedom of worship I had never experienced before, which has had a direct impact on my life and the way I now handle the various situations which come into my life. The Lord has truly become my source of strength and my delight, as I stand in His presence each day as a Royal Priest, ministering to the Father's heart.

Practice these principles regularly in your life and I believe you too will be changed, and you will find yourself in a whole new world of worship.

A FINAL WORD ON LIFESTYLE WORSHIP

This is the end of the study manual on Lifestyle Worship, but it is not the end of your learning experience. Rarely does one read a book and immediately experience a complete change in life; rather learning is a lifelong process, as the principles learnt must be integrated into our lives if we are to reap any benefits from them. Head knowledge alone will not suffice!

The principles outlined in this manual may be used to either increase your knowledge of the Word only, or they may be used to help you experience God in your life on a deeper level. The choice is yours. Great blessings await those who will learn to minister to the heart of the Father as Royal Priests under the New Covenant. This will take discipline and a hunger and love for more of God.

I would encourage you to make the decision to be a daily worshipper and not just a Sunday worshipper. Be bold, be very courageous, step out in faith as your heavenly Father is waiting to receive your worship, and you shall certainly be blessed beyond words as you find a new sense of freedom in your worship experience.

The thought of openly praising God can be a daunting thought for many, we are often conscious of what others might think of us and by doing so are robbed of a great blessing. I encourage you to think only of who you are in Christ; one who has been redeemed by the blood, washed clean, filled with the glory of God, standing righteous before God as His child according to His image, filled with faith, love, joy and peace, for this is who you are!

Child of God, open your heart to the Father, declare and proclaim who He is, rest in Him and rejoice in Him. May the following Psalm become the song of your heart.

Psalm 147 NASB

Praise the LORD! For it is good to sing praises to our God; For it is pleasant and praise is becoming.
The LORD builds up Jerusalem; He gathers the outcasts of Israel.
He heals the broken-hearted, and binds up their wounds.
He counts the number of the stars; He gives names to all of them.
Great is our Lord, and abundant in strength; His understanding is infinite.
The LORD supports the afflicted; He brings down the wicked to the ground.
Sing to the LORD with thanksgiving; Sing praises to our God on the lyre,
Who covers the heavens with clouds, Who provides rain for the earth, Who makes grass to grow on the mountains.
He gives to the beast its food, and to the young ravens which cry.
He does not delight in the strength of the horse; He does not take pleasure in the legs of a man.
The LORD favours those who fear Him, Those who wait for His loving-kindness.
Praise the LORD, O Jerusalem! Praise your God, O Zion!
For He has strengthened the bars of your gates; He has blessed your sons within you.
He makes peace in your borders; He satisfies you with the finest of the wheat.

He sends forth His command to the earth; His word runs very swiftly.
He gives snow like wool; He scatters the frost like ashes.
He casts forth His ice as fragments; Who can stand before His cold?
He sends forth His word and melts them; He causes His wind to blow and the waters to flow.
He declares His words to Jacob, His statutes and His ordinances to Israel.
He has not dealt thus with any nation; And as for His ordinances, they have not known them. Praise the LORD!

For further information regarding this or other materials please visit the author's website: www.globalwordministry.org

The author may also be contacted via email: orlando@globalwordministry.org

APPENDIX

The following is a list of some of the Names of God. These names reveal the nature and character of God enabling us to have a greater understanding and knowledge of God. It is as we know Him that we can love Him more deeply. The more we know God the more we shall be able to offer praise and thanksgiving for who He is and what He has done for us.

I would suggest reading the scripture passage associated with each name to gain a deeper understanding of the origin of the name. Then;

- Praise God for who He is according to His Name.
- Thank Him for all He has done for you according to His Name.

Elohim – Creator & Supreme Ruler

This name is first used in connection with the creation process of the heavens and earth. It reveals God as being the supreme creator of all life form and as being the One who stands as the supreme ruler and judge of all the earth. It reveals God as the Almighty One, the One who has all the power to create something out of nothing, where nothing existed God spoke it into being. Not only did He create but He made all to be perfect and beautiful, and He created man in His own image and likeness. He alone is able to sustain life by His power, providing all that is needed for life.

Scripture Reading:

- Genesis Chapter One
- Genesis 28:10 - 22
- Psalm 102:25 – 27
- Isaiah 40:28 – 29
- Isaiah 41:10

El Shaddai – God Almighty

El Shaddai is first revealed to Abram as the strong and steadfast God of Covenant, the one who initiates a covenant and sustains it, the one who can be trusted to keep His Word and promise, the one for whom nothing is impossible but who can do all things.

Scripture Reading:

- Genesis 17:1 – 8, 15 – 18.
- Psalm 91
- Genesis 48:3 – 4.

Jehovah Jireh – The Lord Will Provide

We serve a God who knows not only our past but also our future; where we will be, what we will be doing, and what provisions we will need. At the time of creation God was both creator and provider for man, He anticipated all man would need to survive and live an abundant life on this earth; He made a beautiful garden called Eden which means pleasure, a paradise for Adam to live in where God had provided everything he would need to live an abundant life.

Jehovah Jireh is first used by Abraham when God provided a ram as a substitute for his son whom he was to sacrifice to God. God knows our needs and is able to make ample provision for us as Elohim is not only the creator of life, but also the one who sustains life. He knows our needs and makes ample provision for His children. Consider what Jesus said;

(Mat 6:31-32 NASB) "Do not be anxious then, saying, 'What shall we eat?' or 'What shall we drink?' or 'With what shall we clothe ourselves?' "For all these things the Gentiles eagerly seek; for your heavenly Father knows that you need all these things.

Scripture Reading:

- Genesis 22:1 – 14

Yahweh – LORD

This is Gods memorial name to all generations and means: I AM WHO I AM. This name would not even be used by the Israelites so great was their respect for Gods Name, instead they used the name Adonai instead meaning Lord. Only the priests involved in the Temple worship would use this name.

Yahweh literally means: "I am the one who was and is and always will be. I am not only the creator of life, but I am life. I am everything you need for life."

Consider Genesis 3:1 – 17 and the setting in which this name is used.

Scripture Reading:

- Genesis 3:1-17
- 2 Peter 1:3
- Revelation 21:6

More Names for your consideration:

a. Jehovah Rophe – The Lord who Heals; Exodus 15:26
b. Jehovah Nissi – The Lord my Banner; Exodus 17:15-16
c. Jehovah Shalom – The Lord is Peace; Judges 6:24
d. Jehovah Roi – The Lord is my Shepherd; Psalm 23
e. Father – Luke 15:11-32, Romans 8:13-17, Galatians 4:4-7